Smack
in the
Middle
of
Life

Smack in the Middle of Life

True Stories and Blessed Aha's

Peggy Treiber DISCARD

Unity House

Unity Village, Missouri

First Edition 2001

Unity House is a publishing imprint of Unity School of Christianity. To receive a catalog of all Unity publications (books, cassettes, compact discs, and magazines) or to place an order, call the Customer Service Department: 816-969-2069 or 1-800-669-0282.

The publisher wishes to acknowledge the editorial work of Raymond Teague and Michael Maday; the copy services of Kay Thomure, Marlene Barry, and Mary Lou Kaltenbach; the production help of Rozanne Devine and Jane Turner; and the marketing efforts of Allen Liles, Dawn O'Malley, and Sharon Sartin.

Cover design and illustration by
Cherie Peltier–Pimento Creative
Interior design by Coleridge Design

Library of Congress Card Number: 2001086832
ISBN 0-87159-271-1
Canada BN 13252 9033 RT

Unity House feels a sacred trust to be a healing presence in the world. By printing with biodegradable soybean ink on recycled paper, we believe we are doing our part to be wise stewards of our Earth's resources.

Dedication

Since I was a cub reporter, my Leo mother
has been nudging me,
"So, when are you going to write a book?"
Okay, Mom. Here it is.
Your believing in me is only slightly less
important than your loving me.

Acknowledgments

Without an audience, this book never would have been written.

You, the reader, are as necessary for this collection as am I, the writer.

In terms of this particular collection, my first audience has been my troubador husband Jeremy, who helps me find my endings. With him, I am "happily ever after." And my writing is better too!

My second audience has been the people I call family—those related to me by blood and friendship. They have read my writings and let me know they laughed and cried throughout my stories. They let me know that what was going on in me was going on in them. We are all one.

I'm glad I've got that one figured out. Thanks, God.

Table of Contents

Contents

Introduction

All I ever needed to know I learned in the dormitory room during my first year in college: we all share the same human conditions.

To this day I remember how surprised I was to learn that my eighteen-year-old roommates also were overly self-conscious, easily embarrassed, and afraid they might fail when they desperately wanted to succeed.

Those late-night confessions were good for my soul, which until then had always thought it was alone on this planet—with its secret fears and tears and dreams.

Each one of us is unique; yet underneath, the similarities are more astonishing than the differences. That's the mystery of life: how we human beings can be one, even when outer appearances put us at six billion and counting.

It's a mystery worth exploring.

And it's one I explore in this book of stories: How can I—and all of us—use values and truths common to most spiritual belief systems when we find ourselves smack in the middle of everyday life?

The vignettes illustrate people going about their daily lives, striving to be authentic, trying to live the Truth, sometimes forgetting how, and then, aha!, remembering God.

Whether we're talking about going to the dentist's office or chauffeuring children in bumper-to-bumper traffic or watching our bodies age, we can live these situations with compassion, humor, understanding and, most of all, an awareness that God is present in every moment.

God makes all the difference in the world.

Living these little moments—and the big ones too—with awareness that God is present transforms life and shifts consciousness.

I've tried to capture these transformations in this book.

I am happy and I am blessed to be able to share them with you.

Thank you.

Keeping Track of

Timelessness

Of time you would make a stream
upon whose bank you would sit and
watch its flowing.
Yet the timeless in you is aware of life's
timelessness,
And knows that yesterday is but today's
memory and tomorrow is today's
dream.
And that that which sings and contem-
plates in you is still dwelling within
the bounds of that first moment
which scattered the stars into space.

—Kahlil Gibran, *The Prophet*

Making soulslaw

I hit the deck running, as usual, after sleeping on and off until 8:30. The night's sleep, begun after midnight, had been interrupted by a short roundtrip drive to school to drop off a daughter. I returned to bed, because six hours of sleep is nowhere near enough for me.

A couple of hours later, my husband—who was dressed and ready for work—glanced at me and saw me stirring. He suggested that I looked like a woman of leisure.

Lying there in bed, hair scattered on my pillow, newspaper on the nightstand waiting to be opened, I was a woman of leisure—for about twenty minutes—until he cleared out of the bathroom.

Then I hit the deck running.

It's a game I play with myself. How much can I get done between the time I wake up in the morning and the time I leave for work in the middle of the afternoon?

Most people work 8-to-5 shifts and come home too tired to do much after spending the first part of their day laboring for money.

My schedule lets me labor first for my family and me, and then—after I've showered, cooked, cleaned, shopped, visited the library, washed and folded clothes and, sometimes even, watched television while curling my hair—I clock in for a job I love that pays the bills . . . and lets me sit!

There is a drawback. Sometimes I need to be a lady of leisure for longer than twenty minutes. Sometimes I need to go slowly. To do things one at a time—well, maybe two at a time. Sometimes I need to spend time in silence. I know this, and yet to cram everything in before it's time to head out, I scurry: a rat in a race of my own making!

That's what I found myself doing on this particular morning. One of the chores on my list for the day was to fix dinner for the family and me— for me to eat at work, them to eat at home.

I poured olive oil into the frying pan and turned on the stove. Then, grabbing some mushrooms and an onion, I sliced them and tossed them into the bubbling oil. Next, I pulled scallops from the freezer and laid the fat, white buttons in the bottom of the pan.

With one dish cooking, I started a vegetarian dish for my daughter. I opened a can of peas, sliced some more mushrooms and tore into a package of angel-hair pasta. Then I put on a pot of water to boil.

Now, with two dishes going, the juggler attempts to add a third to the act.

So, as the pasta water simmered and the scallops sautéed, I turned my attention to the head of cabbage on the cutting board. I wanted to make coleslaw, but was there time? Looking at the clock, I realized I'd been preparing foods for more than an hour—cooking and cleaning as I went. There wasn't a lot of time left in which to chop, grate, and mix. My other job loomed.

Ah well. The slaw needed to be made so that it could be eaten with the scallops. I lifted my knife to make the first cut into the hard, round vegetable. Down it came, against the cutting board, then chop, chop, chop. Chop, chop, chop. Chop, chop, chop.

Hmmm. There was a rhythm here.

Chop, chop, chop. Move the wedges, and chop, chop, chop some more.

I smiled and took a breath. Gee, that felt good.

I breathed again, a little more deeply and became aware that my shoulders had been hunched forward as if anticipating, at any moment now, having to lift a two-ton car off a trapped passenger. Unaware, I had assumed this fight mode when all I really wanted to do was shred the creamy green cabbage leaves.

Chop, chop, chop, move the wedges. Chop, chop, chop.

I scraped the jade shards into a crystal bowl then turned my attention to grating carrots. When the carrots became nubs too small to grate, I popped them into my mouth and savored their cool, sweet crunch. Then I picked up a handful of green onions, lined up their tops, and snipped.

It was at this moment when I noticed that the onion pieces resembled little green *o*'s as they fell from the scissors into the salad bowl. For no reason at all, this delighted me—so much so that I stopped for a moment to study the pattern the dark green circles created against the cabbage.

This one act returned me to the present moment, the moment where the only thing in the world that I needed to do was make coleslaw. Everything else in my mind fell away as the green *o*'s fell, punctuating the cabbage-and-carrot concoction.

I felt like I was in a movie where I was both cameraperson and actor—watching myself play the part of, in this instance, cook. Turning, I glided across the room to the refrigerator for a package of frozen corn. "Chop slaw, carry corn," I said into my imaginary camera, laughing at myself.

The universe had caught my attention, so I watched closely as I dropped the icy, gold nuggets into the bowl. A dollop of mayonnaise, a splash of balsamic vinegar, and all the individual ingredients of the slaw now lay within the confines of the bowl. As I mixed everything together, my spoon hit the side of the bowl and sounded a note not unlike a singing meditation bowl I'd recently toyed with in a store.

But the moment held such presence, such clarity; it didn't have the faraway, other-world feeling of a meditation.

I was here. The bowl was here. The salad was here.

The creating was here. In this moment. Now. Creating is an active, never-ending process, and all I had to do was become aware of it.

That night I called home from the office to chat with my husband, who by now had eaten dinner.

"Did you enjoy the scallops, honey? Did you try the coleslaw?" I asked.

"Excellent," he said. "And the slaw—did you do something differently?"

"Yup," I answered. "I paid attention."

Finding time
within the moment

*W*e're eternal beings. We can only use time as a measure . . . a measure of whether we're living within the moment.

No place is this more apparent than in my kitchen. I can split a bagel, stick it under the broiler and, supposedly to save time, type on the computer in the adjoining room while it toasts . . . and toasts . . . and toasts until the smoke alarm goes off and I remember.

I spend more time scraping away the blackened bread or tossing it to the dog and starting over.

You would think that after five or six, or thirty-five or thirty-six, times of doing this, I'd realize I need to stand at the oven and wait the two minutes it takes to brown the bread.

You don't know me very well.

Instead, I insist on handling this situation by trying to remember that the bagel is under the broiler while I'm flipping through an electronic database. I insist on trying to be within two moments simultaneously.

"Sometimes I can do it," I tell myself.

But in my lucid (translate less stubborn) moments, I realize what's really happening when it seems I can cook and compute at the same time. What's really happening is that my attention is repeatedly shifting from one task to the other.

Once a year I do well in my Formica-topped time laboratory. Once a year I make two batches of apple strudel from scratch. Making this Austrian delicacy entails making my own phyllolike dough, and this requires a big bag of time, a heaping cup of patience, a scoop of dexterity, and several sticks of butter.

I go into this strudel-making session knowing it will take six hours of my life and knowing that my full attention will have to be focused on one goal: turning out these golden pastries layered with apples, nuts, and raisins.

I go into this session accepting these conditions. And so my strudel-making becomes an annual six-hour meditation. (The infrequency of this meditation is dictated by the dangerous number of calories and carbohydrates in this delicious pastry!)

My kitchen, however, does offer me a more regular opportunity to find eternity within the moment. Long ago I purchased a microwave oven to save time. (There's that erroneous concept again!) With a little help from me and a metal spoon, it melted down one day. I threw it out and, for several years, gave no thought to replacing it, despite the pleadings of my children. My kids live in an instant society . . . a fast-food society . . . a society in which nachos are best created in a microwave. I live in that society too, and over time, my resolve—like the microwave—melted.

One day, in the store, I saw an $80 microwave that came with a free itty-bitty coffeemaker. The price was right! I left the microwave with the kids and took the coffeemaker to my office.

One pot later, I understood why it was free.

You've seen those dribble cups meant to be gag gifts? This glass carafe was made by the same company. You can't pour the water into the pot from the carafe without spilling it all over, unless you pour at a speed of approximately ten seconds an ounce.

If you've been paying attention, you can guess how much time I've spent sponging up the puddles of water every time I make a pot of coffee. I told you before that I'm a slow learner.

But this coffee pot's an insistent teacher, and I find I am getting better and better at purposefully pouring the water into the pot. Now when I make a pot of coffee—French roast decaf, please— I'm good to the last drip.

Tempest in a potluck

Anyone who knows me knows that I have a life issue with time. Now this is pretty ironic, I think, because I do believe I am an eternal being, so (with apologies to Tina Turner) what's time got to do with it?

Quite a bit, apparently.

I think it's important to note that I chose a mate who often is oblivious to time. I think he is supposed to be teaching me something about letting go of the next hour in favor of this one. And I think I am supposed to be teaching him a little about accomplishing more this hour and not saving everything for the next.

Over the years both of us have moved in each other's direction, but, sometimes, it seems not enough.

So it's Friday afternoon, ten minutes after five, and he tells me there's a potluck at the Temple at six o'clock. And he needs to be there because he's supposed to welcome the out-of-town teenagers who have driven up to conduct the Shabbat service afterward.

Right.

Not wanting to go to the potluck empty-handed, I jump into the car and speed to the grocery store. Remember now, it's Friday evening, suppertime, and the place is mobbed. I fill my cart with deli salads and a few other items and head for the shortest check-out line I can find.

Upon the register is taped a sheet of paper: "This Line: Paper Bags Only."

Okay, I think, I can handle that.

My cashier, apparently, cannot.

He picks up a bag, shakes it out, pops it open, fluffs it outward from the inside, and places it on the counter. Then he repeats the process with another. And another. And another.

Now, finally ready to scan my groceries, he moves methodically—methodically being my euphemism for slowly. In my assemblage are eight identical packages of ramen. Does my checker know multiplication? Does he understand that it's now ten minutes until potluck? Does he care?

Well, he does care about uncrinkling the wrapper of each ramen package, holding it up to the scanner, listening for the beep, and then balancing it atop the salads in one bag.

"There's a lesson here," I think, and I stay mostly calm, until I put the paper bags into the car and the fourth one bursts, scattering groceries all over the ground.

The only positive in this mess is that I didn't buy eggs.

I throw the items into the backseat and head home.

The acid is bubbling in my stomach, and I'm angry at the bag, the cashier, the husband—and me for being mad.

I tell myself that this is a chance to grow spiritually and emotionally, right here, right now. I tell myself that, but what works is realizing Temple time is traditionally fifteen to twenty minutes later than ordinary time. Given the fact that everybody else is likely to arrive fifteen minutes late, I figure we, too, have a shot at making it there within that framework.

A little calmer now, I get home at 6:05 and see Jeremy coming out. To help unload the car? No, to drive over and pick up his son who's going to the potluck too. I fume as I carry in three bags and half a dozen handfuls of loose groceries.

I spend the next twenty minutes fuming even more and watching the clock. It's 6:30 before they walk in the door to get me and the food, and I am burning. Heartburning.

We drive in stormy nonsilence to the fellowship hall, and the two of them are glad to get out.

I make them carry in the salads, and I slink in through the back, still upset with myself for being upset and upset with my husband for not being upset.

No one pays attention to our lateness. No one cares. Everyone is eating, talking, milling.

Then I overhear a conversation.

The woman who drove the teens in from out

of town has a sick daughter and needs to take her to the motel. But she doesn't know our town, so I find myself volunteering to lead her there in my car.

"But you'll miss your dinner," she protests.

"Not hungry," I reply.

It's not until I'm in the car that I realize the folly of what I've just done. Somehow, in the last half hour, it's turned dark, and I can't see well in the dark.

So now I'm stressing about what's the easiest way to get to the motel, how will I know she's still behind me in the dark, and what will we do if we get separated at stoplights.

What's the lesson here, God?

My guts turn over and squeeze hard; my face flushes. Oh geez, am I going to have to pull over and tell her I'm too sick to drive?

I couldn't stand the embarrassment . . . Better to pass out in the car while driving and wreck than be embarrassed, I decide.

I turn on the radio. Doesn't help. I start singing loudly. Doesn't help.

And then I think to try something more God-oriented. Like prayer affirmations, and between the intestinal spasms and the waves of burning acid rising in my throat, I start spitting out: "I am whole and perfect. I am whole and perfect. I am whole and perfect."

Then I remember a friend whose mother just last week attended her own mother's funeral and, en route home, pulled her car over to the side, had a heart attack, and died.

"I am a healthy child of God." "God within heals me now." "Help me, God, I'm going ditzy." Merging onto the highway, I lose my traveling companion and pull off to the shoulder, wondering how I will find her, how I will get back into traffic.

Paralleling how God works when we get separated, she finds me and slows to let me in.

For the first time since five o'clock, I begin to relax. The beads of perspiration on my forehead evaporate.

Then someone pulls in between us. My hands grip the steering wheel, and through clenched teeth, I sing, "I am a calm, clear center of peace learning to radiate peace every day." "Except today," I add aloud, and start to chuckle.

Laughing at myself is my personal sign from God that I'm going to be okay. Kind of like Noah's rainbow.

The motel's neon sign is within sight. If I lose her now, she'll still get there. But I don't lose her.

I pull in, she steps out, and from the bottom of her heart, she thanks me for leading her.

"I never would have found it," she says.

She has no idea of what was going on in the car in front of her, and for that I'm grateful. These lessons are humbling enough in the company of one's own soul.

Four days later I'm hurrying my son along to

make an 8 A.M. doctor's appointment. We leave the house with seven minutes to spare, and I discover I've left the checkbook at home. Turn around, go back, use up four minutes. We're going to be late.

My guts start to churn when, from deep inside, a little voice sings out: "I am a calm, clear center of peace . . ."

For today, anyway . . .

Staying fourteen forever

$\mathcal{M}$y fourteen-year-old daughter told my husband, one evening while I was at work, that life was over at twenty-one. She said, "You get married, and it's all downhill from there." She figures she has seven years to cram in enough excitement to last a lifetime.

He was upset when he relayed the conversation to me, and I might have been, too, except that her words jarred loose an old memory. As a teenager, I used to put myself to sleep at night by fantasizing grand scenarios for myself in which I was this brave, adventurous, loving, beautiful girl who served as Ambassador of Good to the world. Nations called on me in times of trouble. Adults sought my wisdom and help. Peers wanted me at every party. I could dance, sing, leap tall buildings in a single bound, and I wasn't even eighteen.

Nor was I married.

In fact, every time I tried to push the dream sequence past my teens and into my twenties, through college years and into marriage, the image turned black and white, leaving me with a picture of a young married woman pushing a baby carriage and knowing this was supposed to be making her happy and fulfilled.

My daughter's comment brought me full circle.

My first thought was that I must not be demonstrating a very exciting life. This I dismissed immediately upon realizing that raising two teenagers—two teenagers who liberally express their individuality in words and actions, loud words and dramatic actions—is a life adventure that could propel a parent clear into sainthood.

Add a husband, a family business, another full-time job, work in the church and temple, evenings out with friends, and gee, are we having fun yet?

Plenty of times, my children have heard me say, "I may be harried, overworked, and taken for granted, but I'm never bored." My life's plot is full of exciting adventures, all right—but the adventures are like run-on sentences. I'm in the middle of one, thinking about what I have to do to prepare for the next, and I miss the pleasure of the event at hand.

I want pauses in between the episodes.

If I could just slow everything down and savor each paragraph while I'm in the middle of creating it, my life would be exactly as I'd imagined it once upon a teenaged time: brave, adventurous, loving, and beautiful.

You know, I like mothering teenagers. I like cooking. I even enjoy washing clothes. I like to participate in community projects. My editing job satisfies both the left and right sides of my brain. I think it's sheer bliss to successfully decode my husband and share a weekend on the same wavelength.

Can't my daughter see this? Or does she see only a blur?

"God," I implore, "give me periods to separate the sequences, or at least some semicolons."

God answers, "Practice tunnel vision!"

"Tunnel vision?" I ask incredulously.

"Yeah, and breathing."

We chitchat a little longer, and I begin to understand.

I can choose to put on blinders so that I can concentrate on only the activity at hand. Squeeze it. Taste it. Say thanks and then take a deep breath, or a couple of them, before moving on. Let the breaths serve as punctuation marks. Let the sentence carry the meaning.

Altogether, they make up my life story. And it's been full of adventure, but I couldn't have known that at fourteen.

And so, I understand now where my daughter (and the fourteen-year-old I once was) is coming from. From the moment.

At fourteen, you find it natural to live in the moment. You're graced with the gift of tunnel vision. Your boyfriend's broken up with you, and sobbing, you know you'll never fall in love again.

Your best friend just hung up on you, and you fear she'll never call back.

That khaki pair of pants on sale for $19.99 is sold before you get back to the store; will there ever again be such a bargain?

Are girlfriends coming over to spend the night? You'll not talk of school, unless it's to mention this cute guy who works at the video store and is in your brother's math class.

At fourteen, you feel your feelings all the way . . . all within the moment . . . all moment by moment. You can't imagine what it would be like to be anything but a teenager.

You're in your moment, and that's as far as you need to look. Find the moment, and you'll find all the meaning and excitement a heart could want.

The numbers don't matter. Find the moment and you can stay fourteen forever.

Life: No strings attached

The only empty table that morning in Rick's Iron Skillet was smack in the middle of the room, so that's where we sat, my friend and I. Rick's is the archetypal country diner—with daily specials, an endless cup of coffee for seventy-five cents, and a waitress who calls everyone "Hon."

As the farmers, the workers on their way to the wheel plant, and the salespeople from the used-car lot across the street talked about sports, the weather, and politics, my friend and I sat down to breakfast and two hours of hot black coffee, the approximate time we spend every couple of months hashing out our lives.

Husbands, sons, daughters or daughters-in-law, coworkers, friends, and God all are fair game for conversation, laughter, tears, and prayer. I'm sure the apple-cheeked guy in the John Deere cap across the room is curious when my tears fall, and it takes the waitress about five coffee re-fills to get used to the idea that we'll be around a while.

On this particular day, I'm bugged. My eldest

has decided to take another day off from work, and I am bothered by his propensity for nonproductivity. His current economic theory is that he should make just enough money to pay his bills, which at eighteen are minimal, and keep himself in fast food and gasoline. His new employer has a "work-when-you-want" policy, and my boy has quickly adapted. I'm bothered by this change in his work habits and bothered by being bothered.

My friend agrees to be bothered too, and, for the next thirty minutes, we chew on what's really important in life. How much productivity do we want for our kids? And what kind of productivity are we talking about here? Better yet, what role does productivity play in our spiritual lives?

She and I come to an agreement that he can choose his own level of economic productivity so long as I, his mother, don't bail him out. She agrees that I can, however, continue to slip him an occasional five dollars and let him raid the family refrigerator. We laugh and move on to other subjects.

Later, after we have hugged each other goodbye, my earlier preoccupation with my son's productivity slips into Higher gear, and I realize that what is going on is not as much about my son as it is about me.

This stuff with my son has been trying to get my attention—my energy—focused on figuring out my own feelings and values about productivity:

how much I want, what kind I want, what role it plays in my spiritual life.

Hmmmmm.

I thought it had to do with him not doing enough, but what this anxiety also is about is me doing more than enough and, in the process, not enjoying it.

My son seems to be living the way he wants, every day. My perception is that I get to live the way I want only after I've managed to shower and dress, chauffeur my daughter to school, wash dishes, fold clothes, clean out the litter box, pick up prescriptions, fix dinner, politely decline the telemarketers' fabulous offers, prepare federal tax reports for the family business, shop for groceries, exercise at the gym, and then head out for an eight-hour shift at the newspaper where I work.

That's my perception.

And yet, "Do I really want to do less?" I ask myself. Which would I not do? I begin to think it's more that I want to enjoy doing all these things at the time I am doing them.

Some, perhaps, I can let go of. My son can go pick up his own prescriptions. And if I discover there's no milk for breakfast, maybe I can feel free to let my daughter eat her cereal dry, without judging our whole mother-daughter relationship by that single act.

And therein lies the crux: So much of the reason for what I do has to do with me judging me. Am I a good enough mom, wife, friend, daughter? "Well, of course I am," my whole Spirit calls out. And yet, there's been a shadow in my head that taunts: "Maybe not. You could do more . . ."

How much more is good enough?

I fear the answer is like the dishes. You rinse and wash and dry and put away, and there's still a dirty glass in the bedroom.

So I compromise and try to do enough of everything that comes my way to muffle this nagging voice that says if I stop listening to it, I will become a lazy, worthless bum.

Where did that come from?

Is that what my son is mirroring for me: some subconscious belief that we have to buy our space here on Earth with time and sweat and pain? Maybe it's time to remember—again—that my life here is a divine gift, no strings attached. And my only task is to remember that I am an expression of God.

I've always been disconcerted by the story of Martha and Mary in Luke, Chapter 10, when Jesus, who has been invited to Martha's home for dinner, gently chides Martha for doing too much at the expense of being who she really is, a child of God.

Martha was trying to prove that she was a good hostess, and she was not letting herself take joy in the role she'd chosen to play. As Martha worked to take care of everybody, making sure the table was set, the dinner was hot, the drinks were poured, Mary simply sat, glorying in Jesus' company:

"Martha welcomed him into her home. She had a sister named Mary, who sat at the Lord's feet and listened to what he was saying. But Martha was distracted by her many tasks; so she came to him and asked, 'Lord, do you not care that my sister has left me to do all the work by myself? Tell her then to help me.' But the Lord answered her, 'Martha, Martha, you are worried and distracted by many things; there is need of only one thing. Mary has chosen the better part, which will not be taken away from her.'"

Mary understood that being in the company of Spirit is our highest work, possible only when we become aware that we are expressions of God.

I don't know if my son understands this of himself or not, but nevertheless, he's reminding me of who I am—and that just being who I am is more than good enough.

Taking my time-outs in the car

Being cooped up in an automobile is a stressful proposition for me. I don't like to drive. I don't like to wait. I do both when I'm behind the steering wheel. It almost feels like a punishment. And yet, some enlightened moments have come flying through my windshield.

A pair of stories. First one: He was riding the bus home from St. Louis, where his van broke down. He wanted me to pick him up in Joplin. It meant I had to drive in the middle of the night, two hours there and two back. I don't see well at night, so driving is difficult, but he had an ace up the sleeve of the one shirt he'd taken. He was my husband.

At 10 P.M. I hit the road and breezed through towns where streets were lit and landmarks familiar. It was later, in the country on two-lane roads with faded pavement stripes, that I began to feel pressure in my left temple.

Then I began to think about how I had no idea where the Joplin bus depot was, or if it was even open. Many small-town depots are afterthoughts, tacked on to diners or gas stations that close when normal folks sleep. Now my temple throbbed.

A tractor-trailer rig whizzed past. It was definitely time to pray.

"Ommmmm . . . Namahhh . . . Shivayaaaaa. Ommmmm . . . Namahhh . . . Shivayaaaaa." Chanting the mantra, I marveled at how I could simultaneously drive, read signs, sing (almost on key), and still worry about whether I'd find the Joplin turnoff. Even so, the pain abated, and my mind began to clear. Enough to notice the changing road smells. The greasy fried-chicken smell of fields fertilized with poultry litter. The mushroomy smell of the woods by the river. The sharp perfume of hay-mown fields. Each segment of the trip carried its own fragrance base and provided something to concentrate on besides the darkness.

When my husband stepped off the bus, he found me in almost good humor, despite the lateness of the hour. He drove us home. I slept.

That's one story. Second one: I promised the teenager I'd pick him up from his Taco Bell job to save him the forty-five-minute walk home— if he used the saved time to do homework. He agreed. I arrived promptly and saw that the drive-through line had nine cars lined up, waiting on tacos and burritos and whatever else the Chihuahua barked up. "Yo quiero Taco Bell!"

Obviously, the teen was going to be late getting off, leaving me to sit, twiddling thumbs in the parking lot, listening to the cars and trucks whiz by. A constant whoosh of traffic. It was, I mused, not unlike the constant whoosh of thoughts speeding through my head, weaving in and out of lanes, sometimes honking, often running into each other, and occasionally stalling out. The comparison made me smile and helped me remember better ways to spend these car-bound moments.

I closed my eyes and breathed in, held the breath, and then, mouth open, breathed out. I kept the tip of my tongue behind my upper teeth. I did this again. And again. And again.

And then I realized the tree frogs were singing. They had been all along, but the clatter and chatter of cars and cogitations had masked them.

I could even hear the metal clasp on the rope of the flag pole softly clanging in the night breeze.

Opening my eyes, I looked inside the restaurant and spied the ceiling fans turning round and round, spinning shadows onto walls. It felt like I was watching a movie being played at a speed slow enough for me to catch all the minute details the director so painstakingly included . . . details that could be appreciated only by the viewer who turns off her own mind long enough to notice.

I let myself take it all in, uninterrupted by commercials, and when the young man opened the car door a quarter of an hour later, he startled me.

He apologized for my having to wait.

"No problem. It was my pleasure," I said. And I meant it.

As a friend likes to tell me, "It's all entertainment!"

Perhaps, I realized, the ticket to a front-row seat is a quiet mind. And maybe, time-outs in the car.

Vacation is the journey, not the destination

They'd taken their children from Boston to Los Angeles, from Toronto to New Orleans. Combinations of kids, anywhere from one to four of them at a time. Given the high cost of flying, most of the time they'd driven.

The children, in fact, had some of their first driving experiences on lonely stretches of Route 66, and the oldest took the clan on a tour of the Painted Desert shortly after getting her learner's permit.

The point of the trip always had been to get to a place where the extended family was reuniting, and get there as quickly as possible.

The point was to get out of the car!

Well, now the children were old enough to refuse to get into the car for days of driving, but the couple still needed to attend to family in distant places.

So they pulled out the map and plotted a route that would take them from the heart of the United States to the windy city of Chicago. No matter which way, the verdict was in: close to twelve hours, including rest stops.

She prepared by going to the library and checking out an audiotaped book on personal growth. He stopped by the grocery store and bought celery, apples, and sunflower seeds. She made a cream-cheese-and-salmon dip and washed out the cooler.

He packed the shampoo and toothbrushes. She added clothes, set the alarm, and the next morning, they hugged their sleepy teenagers good-bye and left.

The sun was coming up, the leaves were beginning to turn, and they knew by sundown they would be with relatives not seen in more than a year. Now it was just a matter of watching the clock tick off the minutes, the highway markers count down the miles.

They watched. And watched. And watched.

They talked. They sat quietly.

She closed her eyes and basked in the sunshine.

He searched the radio for a baseball game.

Later, she put in the tape, and they listened.

He stopped the tape so they could talk about what the narrator had just said.

At lunch, they missed the exit in downtown St. Louis and laughed that, once again, a tour of the Arch would have to wait for another trip.

They ate omelets in the middle of the afternoon, near Springfield.

They counted cornfields across Illinois.

Then she popped a music cassette into the player, and they accompanied Peter and Gordon and Chad and Jeremy. He harmonized, she sang melody.

About forty miles outside of Chicago, the traffic stopped. Construction work was squeezing two lanes into one during rush hour.

They'd been driving ten hours, making good time, and now, they couldn't even drive ten miles an hour.

There was no exit. They could only wait. And wait.

She turned to him and stroked the back of his neck to release the tension. He smiled. It was okay.

At the very moment that they finally reached the city limits, a song came on the oldies radio station to which they were tuned. By the '70s rock group—Chicago! They turned to each other and laughed at the serendipity.

And that's when she knew, and he did too, that they had just finished the best part of the trip. The vacation part of the trip. The part where they put aside phones and schedules and jobs and family and simply existed, side by side, enjoying each other's company. Enjoying their own company.

The vacation would stop to allow time to re-unite with family, sightsee, try new foods, explore the city. Fun stuff, but not akin to the "vacating" they had just enjoyed. It would be resumed in a few days on the drive home.

And, maybe, they would find a way to make it last a little longer by stopping in St. Louis to spend the night. Maybe, this time, they would even ride the cart to the top of the silver Arch.

Or, maybe they would just turn on the radio and cruise the town.

Keeping the Sabbath

The easiest time for me to center my thoughts and control my attitude is when I go away. I kick back and relax just as soon as I cross the county line.

There's something about leaving town. Maybe it has to do with "town" being the physical center of two teenagers, nine pets, a family business, a job of my own, and more.

"Out of sight, out of mind" is the attitude I throw into my bag when I head out. If I'm hundreds of miles away, I really cannot get my son to his job on time, fix clogged toilets, or buy groceries. I let go and let somebody else . . .

Meditating is a going away without leaving town, I guess, but when I open my eyes and look around, there are the same dirty dishes, the same pile of clothes waiting to be folded, and the same cat with feline leukemia crying for his medication as before I closed my eyes.

I may be a little calmer as I head for the sink, but by the time I'm trying to pair up an odd number of white socks, I'm baaaack! I find I can live more in the moment when the moment doesn't involve bills and schedules and parenting.

Sabbaths offer another way to go away without having to drive farther than church or temple. I think that's why God insisted on a day of rest for Her/Himself and for us human creations.

If just one day a week, we can live the majority of our minutes in the present moment—aware of what's happening now and not concerned with Monday morning—maybe over time we can develop a skill that will serve us all weeklong.

It takes more than a couple hours of worship for some of us to develop this skill. It certainly takes more than that for me. It takes a day trip, at the very least, and so a recent Sabbath found me traveling with husband and friends to a favorite lake in another county. The car was full of rafts and sunscreen, hot dogs and baked beans, iced tea and cold, sweet watermelon.

We drove along winding highways, uphill and down, until we spotted the tiny road that would take us to the community of Beaver, population 95, and home of a wooden, one-lane suspension bridge that crosses Table Rock Lake.

We parked, unloaded, and I sat there waiting for friends to blow up their rafts with an electrical pump long after I'd filled mine with air from my lungs. Later, when I lay upon the water, I smiled to think that it was my air that held me up.

Far away my son's alarm clock was waking him for work. But I was here, and time was not.

Rolling off my raft into a mix of warm and cool water currents, I floated face down, arms

and legs splayed loosely, not breathing. I remembered hearing that the moments of stillness between breaths are the times in meditation when
we are closest to God.

Not wanting to be too close, I flipped over
onto my back and inhaled deeply. Aaah. The water
held me up, even without the raft; and with my
ears submerged, I could hear my soft breathing.
It reminded me of the placenta sounds heard
within my uterus when children lived there.

"I am on my way to becoming a born-again
mystic," I chuckled.

The fat, white clouds moved across the sky,
and from my vantage point, my focus was singular:
sky was all I could see. I watched the clouds shap-
ing and reshaping. I felt the sun and shadow.

Later, I rode home, relaxed, refreshed, and
reddened—despite the diligent use of sunscreen.
And when the trash needed to be taken out, the
drooping flowers watered, and the cat given his
medicine before I could bed down for the night,
the sunburn was a gentle reminder that I had
created myself this day a glorious memory made
from many single moments.

Like God, I saw that it was good.

In no time at all

There are moments in our lives when we have the chance to glimpse eternity. Not all of these moments are of the panoramic sunset variety. Some are downright bizarre.

Understand that I'm defining eternity as timelessness.

In human form and not yet having shaken free of time's shackles, I am a good slave to Master Time, bowing and scraping and begging for more.

But I have my moments.

When I was in California last month, I woke up before dawn and drove to Bodega Bay to taste the salt water. In the early morning light on a damp and foggy beach, I stood, arms stretched out to the ocean. And as the waves left a ribbon of foam at my feet, I could sense my infinity within the ceaseless rhythms.

These are the eternal moments I especially like.

I get others too.

Like the last five seconds of the college's basketball game—when time stopped. Literally. I knew we had lost the game. And then, fate stepped in—and a referee—and turned a few seconds into more, and my team came back to improbably tie the game and earn five minutes of overtime.

That kind of timelessness is hard for me to stand, so I left the arena and listened to the game on the radio while driving home.

What seemed like an eternity later, my team won, and clocks went back to ticking sixty seconds to the minute, sixty minutes to the hour.

Then there was the recent afternoon when my daughter called from her dad's house to say he'd been taken to the hospital by ambulance. Time stopped, and my heart skipped a few beats too.

It was as if there'd been no time at all between our divorce and now. Apparently a piece of legal paper isn't sharp enough to sever the ties that bind—even when the ties are too tight.

Everything turned out okay, but in those first moments after her call, I understood the eternal connection among us all.

Maybe the trick is to have these moments of timelessness one right after the other.

Maybe that's what heaven is. Maybe I'm not quite ready yet.

2

Sorting Out

Appearances

All the world's a stage, and all the men and women merely players: They have their exits and their entrances;
And one man in his time plays many parts.

—William Shakespeare, *As You Like It*

Watching windows

The windows in the new home we are building are open to the air right now. Framed-in, glassless rectangles, they offer an unencumbered panorama of trees, ravine, creek, squirrels, and birds.

The sun streams through them. The wind blows through them. The snowflakes dance around them, settling on the sill supports.

Soon these windows will have double-paned glass.

Later will come miniblinds and, maybe, insulated draperies because these windows face north.

Each night when the builders leave the house for the day, I show up to sit on the plywood subfloor and gaze out the open windows.

This is my favorite phase in building a structure: when its shape is defined but the world shows through.

I thought about these windows when I was recalling a friend's advice to let absolutely everything—what we label good and what we label bad—flow through us without judgment. Without attachment.

I thought about how my windows—with glass or without—don't judge the weather or the views that flow and show through them.

It is I who have taught myself to open them wide for sunshine and shutter them tight against the storms.

It is I who have labeled warm air "good" and cold air "bad," but even I change my judgments in August.

I didn't always judge. I, too, was as open as my windows when I was "under construction."

But my human condition made it necessary for me to learn that hot can burn and cold can freeze.

Now, my spiritual condition assures me that letting go of judgment will allow me to better reflect the Light within.

Now I am seeking to take down the blinds and pack away the labels.

Now I want to sit on the subfloor of my soul and enjoy the view.

Form over function

Sometimes change has to happen from the outside in.

Sometimes form has to precede function. And feeling.

A couple of years ago, my aunt, in mourning after the deaths of both her husband and my dad, was preparing for the Christmas holidays. She said to me, as she decorated the tree, wrapped the presents, and ground cranberries for the traditional cranberry-orange relish, "Sometimes you have to let the motions carry you through."

My children's grandmother used to tell their dad, "You have to keep on keeping on." Even when it doesn't make sense. Even when everything feels out of control. Even when the ground is shifting.

It was advice from the older generation, and for a long time, it didn't resonate with me.

But life provides lots of shake-ups. Lots of opportunities to "get" the advice my elders proffered. Mostly, however, I've responded to these opportunities by stressing out, even though I knew that this reaction was as stupid as running back into a building after a magnitude-7 earthquake.

It's not that I haven't tried to manage stress, make friends with it, or at least, come to terms with it. Oh, the number of times I've tried to de-stress myself from the inside out . . . but I've been unable to sustain a feeling of calm.

The calm comes. And it goes.

I turn around and see myself and am sur-prised that I don't seem to be able to live from my soul, and not my personality, for more than min-utes at a time. Ultimately, my stress-management technique has been to grit my teeth, clench my fists, and "bull" my way through. It reminds me of the person who never learns to swim, who kicks and chops and churns through the water rather than gliding.

Guess what? Our bodies can handle stress-ful events in such an inefficient manner for only so long, and then they themselves become the lesson.

For years my blood pressure has been at the upper end of normal, and I've watched it. I would go to the pharmacy, sit down at the blood-pressure machine, stick my arm into the gray plastic sleeve, and press "Start." Then I would take a deep breath, close my eyes and imagine myself float-ing on water, and wait.

If the numbers came out at 120 over 80, I was happy. If they came out at 130 over 90, I could live with that. But when they started coming out higher, I started to be concerned. I lost some weight, and still they didn't come down. I started walking. I added three daily capsules of garlic to the regimen and became a "borderline" case.

Anytime I saw a blood-pressure machine, I approached it fearfully, defeating any chance of a normal reading. After a while, I just stopped checking it. I figured the walking and the working out would melt away the pounds.

Then, in the doctor's office for a broken foot, I had an incident of high blood pressure that scared me and alarmed the doctor. She put me on medicine, and I agreed, provided I could get off it if my numbers dropped along with the rest of my weight. Okay, she said.

Fifteen years ago her predecessor had shied away from medicating me, telling me to work on it myself, recognizing that the divorce stuff I was going through then was probably a big reason my pressure was high. The readings improved, and ever since, I'd made it a badge of honor that I wasn't taking the little green and yellow diuretic pills. Now, here I was filling the prescription, and feeling like a failure. This was not acceptable.

Then I remembered my aunt. "You have to go through the motions." Maybe, just maybe, I should stop trying to nag and "guilt" my way into relaxation and instead adopt some outer techniques that, eventually—and with the weight loss—would transform my insides. A kind of behavior-modification approach.

When I asked the Universe what techniques I should try, I remembered a conversation I'd had with a friend this spring. We were talking about whether it was possible, in this day and age, to do one thing at a time. Start a task, finish it, and move on. The idea was so incredible that I suggested we change the premise to no more than two things at a time. "Three" she said, laughing. We parted and returned to doing five and six things at a time, but with greater awareness. I came to realize that not only do I do several things at a time, my mind is already working on rescheduling the dentist appointment while my hands are in the dishwater, the computer is running, and my curling iron is heating up in the bathroom.

I never finish a task and celebrate its completion. I never finish a task and simply take a deep breath. No wonder my blood-pressure readings are a roller-coaster affair.

I decided to make a pact with myself. I would take the little pill every day, and I would bless it, grateful for its help. I would consider it as necessary a part of my healing as the cane I used to support my broken foot. And I would not use the broken foot as an excuse to stop exercising, but rather I would switch to water jogging in the swimming pool. And every time I passed by the candy machine at work, I would think about which I wanted more: chocolate or diuretic pills. It was a no-brainer.

Most important, I would not finish whatever I was doing without recognizing it as an ending and an accomplishment, before moving on to whatever else needed my attention. I would create a break between the tasks and not slur them all together.

That's the pact. I'm not doing it perfectly, and I don't know when my numbers will improve— weight or pressure. But I've made friends again with both the scale and the blood-pressure machine because, like the pills, they are helpful crutches.

For years I've known that I needed to relax, not stress out so much. It took my body to get my attention. Sometimes the outer leads the way to the inner.

It's immaterial

I had some guidance recently that I was taking life too seriously. As if it mattered.

This new home in which I move to the music of squirrels and crickets and birds . . . could I give it up? My children, safe and secure within its walls and still within my arms' reach . . . could I give them up?

My spouse, my parents, my friends.

My glassware. My Lizwear. My weight. My hair. My thoughts. My photographs. My writing.

Could I give them up?

So here I am, the perennial worrywart and collector, now being guided to a place where nothing matters, because, I am gently reminded, Spirit is the substance of everything material. The essential stuff is immaterial, and the meaning of anything is defined by whoever's taking the measurements.

When I was a young adult, I was determined to figure out the meaning of life so that I could cross that task off "My Life Work List" before I turned forty.

Back then I thought life had a meaning that was definable and absolute, and if I could just figure it out, I'd be all set.

Well, I'm past forty, and my inner guide has just informed me I'm going to have to figure out how to have a good life without any meaning. Because, almost everything to which I've assigned meaning—other than acts of love—is perishable, transitory, material.

House. Possessions. People.

Go ahead, enjoy them here, in this moment, now. But if they go, let them.

The love remains. The energy remains. The Divine Connection remains.

That's what matters, even if it is immaterial.

Altering our costumes

Driving through town on a spring evening, I spied a tall, gray rat with a giant head, waggling a red-gloved hand at me and all the other passing cars. I waved back.

I recognized the rat immediately. It was the Chuck E Cheese's mascot trying to draw in the pizza-and-arcade-game crowd by standing on the curb, waving at passersby.

Fortunately, my kids have outgrown Chuck E Cheese's and rarely beg me anymore for quarters to buy tokens. (Now they beg for dollars for Taco Bell and the movies!), so I was able to wave freely and keep on driving, which got me to thinking.

Here I am waving at a costumed employee, who is probably raking in all of six bucks an hour, and accepting this person as a giant rat!

That's right. It was a rat waving at me. A smiling rat—reason enough to beware. And a big one. My eyes told me it was a rat, and the rest of me agreed. Rodent was the outer manifestation, and I accepted that in an instant.

Further down the road, I thought about what it really was—a human being inside a rat costume. I wondered if the individual was male or female. A teenager working to make money for gas and clothes? An older fellow moonlighting to make a little extra money for the family?

Did the person inside the big, gray body like the suit he'd been given to wear for a few hours? Did he tousle the tuft of hair between the ears and wish that it was thicker?

Was she relieved to know she would be able to take it off when dusk came and it would be too dark for passing cars to see her?

Okay, I'll admit that my mind takes me to some strange places when I'm driving, but there was an analogy inside that varmint.

Every morning, when I awaken from the gloriously formless state of dreaming, I look down and find myself somehow tangled up again in this flesh costume. Some days the costume seems too big. It pulls me down as I move through the hours. Some days it kinks in funny places and hurts me when I wear it. And I notice that the longer I wear it, the more wrinkled it becomes.

If I pass people on the street while I'm wearing this heavy head and these blue-veined hands, they usually nod politely. I'm thinking that what they see is how my face has tanned unevenly because of the wraparound sunglasses I wear.

"Look inside me," I want to call out. "This isn't all I am. Look closer."

But all they see is that my hair looks like I slept in it.

I glance back and tend to see the same.

Our passing comes and goes in an instant, and there's not enough time to register that the costumes are hiding something deeper. Instead, what we see are face and eyes and hair and skin: coordinates of the human garment.

I have to close my eyes to peer under the mask.

It's hard not to notice how some masks are prettier than others. If we have one of these, is it harder to watch it wear out? Our culture makes money offering ways to alter our costumes: dyes and bleaches, implants and reductions, liposuction, plastic surgery, skin abrasions, and chemical peels.

For my part, I pop multivitamins and drink green tea made with filtered water to keep my costume's seams as tight as possible. My sister uses a treadmill daily to work on her costume. My brother tore his costume in several places, riding his bicycle in the Sierra Nevada mountains and had to mend it before he could ride again. My mother let a surgeon open up her costume and replace the broken parts.

A year ago my father took his costume off. We burned it.

It's still hard not to have him standing on the curb, waving at me as I drive up to visit. But he's doing better than six bucks an hour now. He flies the friendly skies, not even needing a senior discount ticket.

Without the cumbersome head, and all the rest, it's easy to be everywhere at once. No wonder Jesus never worked for Chuck E Cheese's. These costumes cramp one's style.

But it's a living. And in a few more decades, when I turn in my costume, I think I'll like the lighter, airier me well enough to wonder why I ever worried so much about this flesh fashion statement that I wear now.

The Truth will set you free

The young woman was in her twenties when a friend came to her with news that she had uterine cancer. The woman wanted to be supportive and prayerful of and for her friend, but at that time in her life, she was not quite sure how to reach God with petitions.

Actually, that was not her only dilemma.

Sharing her fears and hopes surrounding her friend's disease and recovery, the young woman talked to her own parents. And they said that they did not believe her friend had cancer. They said her friend's parents had tried to talk to the doctors, but the friend refused permission. There was something "funny" about the whole affair, they said.

What they said made sense to the young woman—reached her brain, logged in, and raised a lot of doubts about whether her friend was being truthful or not—and the young woman did not want to feel taken for a sucker, duped. She wrestled with this. She questioned whether she could trust her friend to tell the truth.

The truth, she was sure, would make everything clear.

Within a week she knew the truth. It became one that would serve her throughout her life—whenever she remembered it.

A couple of decades later a young man came to her with news that his girlfriend's family had a chance to move into a government-subsidized apartment—if the family could come up with the money to pay off an old electric bill and pull together a deposit. She listened intently, for the young man was her son.

His girlfriend's mother worked cleaning motel rooms for barely more than minimum wage. She was single, and in addition to her sixteen-year-old daughter, she also had an eight-year-old son. No father was in the picture. No child-support check was in the mail.

The woman pondered this and wondered about the truth of the matter.

"How much does she need?" she asked the young man, who had promised to pay her back from his own money made at his own six-bucks-an-hour-flipping-hamburgers job.

"Could you loan me $100?" the young man asked.

She paused for a moment.

"No," she replied. "I'll not loan you the money. I'll give you the money, and you can give them the money. And when you give them the money,

I want you to tell them that once someone came to me and said: 'Here, I appreciate the work you do. Have this $100, no strings attached.'

"Tell them that some day they will have an opportunity to help someone, and in doing so, they can continue the chain. We are all connected. Remember that."

The young man hugged her hard, and she marveled at what a good technique this would be for bill collectors—hugging people every time they brought in a payment.

When her son had gone, the woman sat beside her husband, who had agreed with her about the money. But now he raised the question of whether the family was being straight with their son: would the money be spent on the utility bill and deposit? He hoped the family had not pulled the wool over their eyes or that the daughter did not see their son as a ticket out of a poverty-stricken life.

It was funny when he said it, and they both laughed at the absurdity of a hamburger flipper being mistaken for a sugar daddy.

Still, a doubt reached her brain and logged in. Had she done the right thing? She wrestled with this. Could she trust this family to tell her son the truth? Had she been duped?

Aaahhh. This was familiar. She remembered. It was not the truth about the family's situation that she needed. It was not the ability to trust in somebody else. The truth had nothing to do with the other person and everything to do with her.

She only had to be true to who she was.

Twenty years ago she'd realized that, ultimately, the truth about her friend's physical condition did not matter. The friend needed support and love, and the only real question was whether she would give it.

Her son's friends needed money, and the only real question was whether she and her husband would share what they had.

We're all connected, she had told her son.

That was the only Truth.

The only way she could have been duped, by her friend or by the friends of her son, would have been if doubts had pulled her away from being the person she knew herself to be, had persuaded her to abandon the Truth of who she was.

The facts of the situation didn't matter at all: she couldn't be duped if she acted from her heart.

Hugging David

"He'll be there," she said. "From everything I've read about people who die, they always go to their funerals. I wonder where he'll be?"

The two of us were headed to a tiny Ozark town to join with David's family in saying good-bye to our friend who had made his transition from the physical to the spirit world.

At fifty-five, David was much too young to die.

If we, as his friends, weren't ready to let go of him, his family's grief was immeasurable.

David was the world's best hugger.

When he took hold of you, you were the only person in his world for that moment. And the next . . . and the next . . . and, sometimes, even the next . . .

His hugs were extended expressions of love.

"Heart to heart, that's how he wanted to hug people," my companion said. "He believed that hugging is how soul touches soul."

To be remembered for your hugs, can there be a better legacy?

His son spoke at the funeral. He said his nephew had been talking about his grandfather in the days following David's passing. About how Grandpa was—and the child had poked his finger toward the sky—up there, in heaven.

"I'm gonna be just like my grandpa," the youngster had said.

What a tribute. What a gift. The child is his own expression of God, but that expression will include David.

For all of us whom David hugged, let our own expressions include him, his son asked. Amen!

David was a tower of strength. He was tall, willowy, and while we knew his health was fragile, we never thought of him as anything but sturdy. When the members of his church would gather, they looked to him for his advice and wit. He was a man whose words and actions were steeped in Spirit. He was a man who emanated inner light.

David, a chiropractic doctor, also was a healer.

David confessed to one of his friends that he wished he could use his healing powers to make himself well.

"Physician, heal thyself," he chuckled.

Then he told his friend something profound.

"I wish I could heal myself, but it really doesn't matter."

It really doesn't matter whether or not our bodies are whole and healthy. David understood that. It's great when they are, and we do what we can to keep them that way, but their health is not the reason we're here.

We're here to express Godlove, and we can do that no matter what covering our souls choose to inhabit.

It's nice to be healthy; it's not necessary. It's not the point.

Hugs are the point. Love is the point. God is the point.

David got that.

He was willing to tell stories on himself of how he "got" that. Over and over, he "got" that. Like the rest of us, sometimes he had to re-remember his essence. It made him all the more endearing.

His funeral brought together a wide assortment of people. Farmers in overalls. Masons in aprons. Doctors. Ministers, traditional and New Thought. And friends from all over. David's funeral was a reunion, full of hugs.

And then there came the proposal—that each of us promise to continue the tradition of David's hugs. To take an extra moment before we pull away. Let our hearts touch. Feel our souls connect.

Do that and David will be there, joining in.

That's the challenge for us, left here in bodies: believe that the relationships we have with friends and families don't stop at death. They just change form.

It's a thin veil that separates the two experiences. A single heartbeat. A single breath.

As prayers were said and many heads were bowed, some of us looked up at the mist-filled sky.

Where Grandpa went, his grandson had said.

My eyes were pulled to the tip-top of an evergreen tree that grew beside what would be his tombstone. I just knew David was hovering there. I turned to my companion, pointed up and smiled. She understood.

David lives.

It's up to us to let his love into our daily lives. To let ourselves be comforted by it. To let ourselves be encouraged by it. To let ourselves be tickled by it—he had a wonderfully wry sense of humor.

He'll stay near, for his wife, his children, his brothers, his grandchildren . . . Even for us.

Not in the physical way that we, inside these arms and legs and heads, would have preferred. But we'll learn a new dimension of love and closeness from his transition. And he'll be helping out on the other side.

One more thing—one of the ministers who spoke said there is nothing we can do for the dead. I don't believe that for a moment. People on the other side are still learning, still moving toward further enlightenment. The same prayers that lift us in human form can lift those who've left their bodies behind. We can pray with David.

It's another way to connect with him.

It's another way to hug him.

The hats we wear

Cleaning out closets recently, I discovered a hat that had been gathering dust since I bought it several years ago. Made of blue denim with a floppy brim and garnished with a pink fabric rose, the hat peered out at me from a pile of caps and gloves.

I remember the day I bought it. My mother and sister were visiting, and we were exploring the local shopping mall.

I spotted the hat, tried it on, made them laugh.

But when I headed toward the cash register, they looked at me like I was out of my mind.

"Are you really going to buy that?" they asked, in diplomatic voices only slightly tinged with dismay.

"Yes!"

I bought the hat. Even tried to wear it a few times. Never for longer than five minutes. Eventually, the hat got lost on the top shelf of my closet. Lost and forgotten until fall cleaning two weeks ago.

Now, holding the soft denim in my hands, I wondered why I could never wear it.

To look at it still made me smile.

In the privacy of my room, in front of my mirror, I tried it on. Who was that looking back?

A woman of whimsy. A child who believes in magic. A soul who trusts that all is right. I am all of these things, some of the time, but mostly in the privacy of my heart. I want to put on the hat, go outside, and dance away my life. Splash through puddles now without fear of sneezing later.

But I fear that people would laugh at me—or, worse, look askance! So, instead, I live a cautious life, looking twice before I cross the street, then moving quickly.

Is it just the natural progression from carefree youth to careful middle age? Do I have to grow old to wear purple and put on a big floppy hat? At least it gives me hope for my old age!

In the meantime, I wrestle with Worry, occasionally breaking free: to drink steaming coffee in the company of dawn; to scuff my shoes through crackly, colored leaves; to turn up the radio volume and sing at the top of my lungs. But, always alone, when no one else can see or hear me.

As for the hat, I tossed it into the costume box and saw it recovered later by my delighted daughter. She wears it everywhere.

I hope she never has to take it off.

Body work

Judaism had the Y2K bug licked. When it celebrated New Year's in September 1999 at the Rosh Hashanah service, its world turned 5760. And I was there when this age-old passage from the New Year's service called to me:

"Our origin is dust and dust is our end.
Each of us is a shattered urn,
grass that must wither, a flower that will fade,
a shadow moving on."

It is a sad passage—especially for 10 o'clock on a warm, bright morning—about the end of the human season. And yet, that warm, bright morning, I began to understand its meaning.

Earlier in the year, in the spring of 1999 or 5759, I had been pondering the aging process, knowing that the decade of my forties was passing quickly. Why, I wondered, do we have to watch our bodies sag and wrinkle and shrink? Why do we have to wither and fade? Why do we have to grow old?

I had always promised myself that, someday, I would begin paying more attention to my body. Take better care of it. On and off over the years, I've walked briskly, but these last few years, it's been more off than on. I learned Tai Chi and loved it, until I stopped doing it and forgot how to execute the balancing dance.

I've never sunbathed, never smoked, rarely drank. I've had a decent diet, if you don't count the sugar. I drank a lot of milk in my teen years, so my bones are strong. And I look younger than my biological age. These are the pluses.

The minuses: I've been too sad, too harried too much of the time (as the wrinkles and the blood pressure attest). I've put on weight. I haven't had a lot of stamina. My exercise regimen has been sporadic.

Adding it up, I decided that "someday" had arrived. It was time to pay my body some much-deserved attention. I would be a new person for the new millennium.

I checked in to the cost and facilities of area health clubs right before Memorial Day weekend. In June I heard about a program for women that offered three free sessions. A sucker for "free," I went three times and was about to sign on the dotted line when I realized the total cost would be hundreds of dollars.

Let me talk this over with my husband, I said, hastily departing.

He and I agreed that a health club not only was cheaper, it would allow both of us to participate, and so, by the Fourth of July, we owned a family membership. A trainer set me up on weights, and I went to my doctor to have a wellness checkup and to get the program okayed. I started working those biceps, triceps, hamstrings, abs, and more. Lots more.

I even returned to the dentist.

I was going to get my body into the best possible shape. Three days a week, I pushed and breathed and pulled and breathed, grunting all the way. The other days I tried to get in some brisk walking, either outside or on the treadmill at the club.

Back in the summer, when the machines felt strange and the people around me were unfamiliar, I wondered if I would keep it up. It's fall now, and I am. This makes me smile. So, too, does being able to look myself in the mirror and not grimace. Or pulling on a pair of pants that have languished in the closet for two years running.

It's not that I'm not still overweight; I am. But I am doing what I can about the situation. I am being the best I can be, here at a body level. Here and now.

It is wonderful, and yet there are those words from the prayer book.

Is not this better toned body also going to wither and fade?

I've seen the women twenty years my senior in the dressing rooms. Their faces are even more wrinkled than mine. Is this a cruel cosmic joke— that we should work so hard to maintain our bodies and still grow wrinkled? That we should live life to the fullest and still die?

Sometimes, however, in the space between pushing sixty pounds forward on the vertical press, then slowly letting it back . . . sometimes, I hear the answer given to me that New Year's morning.

When we, as spiritual beings in this human experience, watch our bodies wrinkle and get old, it is because our Higher Self is asking us to begin to let go of them and our strong attachment to them. This is a gradual process.

We spend the first half of life watching our bodies grow up, wondering at the marvelous feats they could accomplish. We spend the second half watching them fade, grateful for all the magnificent ways in which they serve us still.

And if, in this stage—even as we take care of them, appreciate them, and bless them—we can accept with grace and humor the changes they are undergoing, we can begin to detach.

We will not be needing these bodies in our next level of experience. Even slim, fresh, and unwrinkled, they would weigh us down.

I am a shadow moving on . . . to a new experience where form and gravity are not measured on life insurance tables and there's no $20-a-month automatic checkbook debit for the gym.

Walking the spiritual path at the mall

I'm a mall-walker. I have been, periodically, since my daughter was two months old. I strapped her in the stroller and took off, the wind blowing wisps of her blonde hair up and down and sideways.

Mall-walkers take their exercise early in the morning, before the stores open. I usually arrive a few minutes before 8 and am back home by 9.

I can make a good case for mall-walking. Great exercise in a controlled, smoke-free environment, and there's always someone to smile at. Floors that are smooth and level. Window displays to entertain. Music piped in so it floats down from the ceiling.

Some days the music is instrumentals I do not know; some days it's rock and roll, and my gait is just a little faster.

Then there are the great smells: chocolate-chip cookies baking, coffee brewing, and leather purses and belts begging to be bought.

Ten years ago, when I started mall-walking, I was one of the youngest there. That's changed. Some of the stores also have changed, but the exercise remains the same. My daughter is in school now so I walk alone.

I've learned to do a very fast walking meditation—if I can keep from checking out the store windows. When I can, I often end up in deep nonthought, until I almost bump into someone.

That's what happened to me a few weeks ago. Just in time, I looked up to see this short, solid man coming at me.

"Hello!" I gasped, veering right.

"Hello," he answered in a voice a little raspy, a little gruff.

Not a regular walker, I thought to myself. His square body was built to move things: boxes . . . tables . . . whole stores! I could tell by the way he was dressed in work clothes. The kind that companies issue you—dark, polyester pants and a shirt in tan or gray or green.

His zippered jacket covered up any name patch on his shirt, and I didn't give him another thought. Back to walking.

Most days I walk three times around the perimeter of the mall, which measures almost two miles and takes me about twenty-five minutes.

Toward the end of my third round that day, I noticed that the music had changed.

Except, it hadn't changed exactly . . . the ceiling music was the same, but there was another music emanating from the shiny black baby-grand piano in the food court.

Incredibly beautiful music wafted down around my shoulders. It soared and dipped and spun. Angels could have danced upon the chords.

I quickened my pace to turn the corner, eager to see who had lifted the black cloth that usually cloaks the piano until noon—when an entertainer plays daily for the lunch crowd.

There, bent over the keys, oblivious to the ceiling music, unaware of the passers-by, immersed in the music he was making, was the worker with whom I'd nearly collided!

He wasn't moving boxes.

I paused to think how quickly I had labeled him, put *him* in a box, as if I knew what he was made of.

I'd taken one look at him and subconsciously assigned him a job, personality, and lifestyle. I assumed these things without even realizing that I was assuming them . . . until his passion grabbed me by the lapels and said, "Look at me again!"

How often do I do this? How often do we all?

What if I had bumped into a carpenter from Nazareth? Perhaps I did.

3

Shaping

Awareness

When you desire to eat or drink, or to fulfill other worldly desires, and you focus your awareness on the love of God, then you elevate that physical desire to spiritual desire. Thereby you draw out the holy spark that dwells within.

—*The Essential Kabbalah:
The Heart of Jewish Mysticism,*
compiled and translated by
Daniel C. Matt

Piecing life together

When family comes to share winter holidays, indoor activities are a must. My husband's daughter and her family were driving to our home when I remembered the fun we had a couple of years ago putting together a puzzle in Chicago where they live.

I headed for the store and found a jigsaw puzzle called Faux Real 1000. A painting by Ken Keeley, it looks like a photograph split into a thousand pieces. This one was a shot of the famous Nathan's hot dog stand at New York's Coney Island.

I picked this puzzle because it had the least amount of sky. It just had to be easier to put together than a faux-real landscape—and a lot more interesting.

Before the next two generations arrived, I dumped all the pieces out of the box onto the table and turned them right side up to reveal the coloration and detail of each. Then I sorted through the pile looking for the edge pieces, given away by their perfectly straight sides. Let the games begin . . .

Daughter, son-in-law, and grandson arrived late in the day. By the time dinner was finished, dishes cleared, the baby rocked to sleep, and after-dinner talk well underway, there had been no time for puzzlement. I yawned "good night" and flopped into bed, falling asleep to the murmurs of their conversation.

When I awoke the next morning, the puzzle had a top, bottom, and two sides—and the words *Nathan's Delicatessen* spread across the middle.

Pieces of sky were piled in little mounds outside the puzzle frame, and pieces of people and cars and signs were heaped within.

Each adult specialized in one part of the puzzle: the automobiles, the street lights, the hot dogs, the big Coke cup, the flag, the motorcycle . . . Each found pieces the other was looking for. It was easy to see how some pieces fit: the jogger's leg, the motorcycle handlebars, the flag's stars. Other parts of the puzzle came together more slowly, but they came together.

All of us avoided the blue sky until the very end when there were no more concrete objects to be interlocked.

We tried to address this final phase by creating piles of sky pieces, looking for those with heavy clouds or wispy clouds or no clouds. Mostly, though, putting the sky together was hit or miss. To wit, I would pick up a piece, hold it over every hole, and see if I could find its special niche.

It is at this point that puzzles begin to lose their fascination. I like to know how the pieces fit together, and I like to know now! Often the more patient son-in-law took a piece I could not fit and placed it in short order, but even he was stumped by some.

"This piece just doesn't fit anywhere!" we would squall. We had to put it down while we worked to make sense of the others.

And do you know what? Eventually, every single piece—including the ones we were sure had been mistakenly boxed in this particular puzzle—did fit. Each had a place that could be occupied by no other and each was necessary to create the full faux photo of this New York landmark.

You see, even if we didn't understand how they fit together while we were puzzling over them, the artist did.

And, in the end, he shared his composition with us. Do you think God works that way?

Keys to the Universe: Asking and listening

It's important to ask the question. It's just as important to wait for the answer. This understanding was brought to me by my husband and his car keys.

Frequently I misplace my keys, carrying them in and laying them on the counter with the groceries or on the desk with the mail or in the bedroom with the drycleaning . . . I have to retrace my steps to find them.

I have come to realize that looking for my keys gives me a few minutes between errands. Often I misplace them when I am in a hurry to get somewhere. I see this as the Universe shoving an opportunity at me to pause and be centered. Car keys can offer clues to how the Universe works.

While my husband may never misplace his, he has locked them inside the car. To his credit, he does this rarely and only when we are out of town: at the zoo in Toronto . . . downtown in Minneapolis . . . and at the beach in Miami.

Maybe these incidents occur away from home because at home we rarely lock the car.

After fiddling with coat hangers and calling locksmiths, I developed the habit of asking him, as he got out of the car, "Do you have the keys?" His door was already locked and shut before he answered, but I always waited to close mine until he dangled the keys at me. I ignored his exasperation.

It's been six years since the last lockout, and in the interim, we have journeyed by car or van to Chicago, San Francisco, New York, Cleveland, Washington, and Atlanta without ever once closing the car door before removing the keys. I was beginning to get lax. I still asked the question, "Do you have the keys?" but I would be swinging my door shut as he answered.

Fast forward to a recent trip to Florida: we spent the night in Pensacola, and as we were leaving the car, we each pushed down our buttons.

"Do you have the keys?" I asked as I began to close my door. His was already shut.

"No!" he answered, staccato. I figured he was being sarcastic because he's impatient with my asking, and I continued to shut my door.

"NO!" he shouted. I caught the door at the last moment and pulled it open to spy keys hanging from the ignition.

"Oh," I sighed, disaster averted. And then the

Light! Maybe if I'm going to ask the question, just maybe I should wait for the answer.

I wondered about the more cosmic implications of this. I often question the Universe about the daily bread of my life and then complain when I don't get a fresh baked loaf of rye immediately. Maybe I expect a certain answer, and if I get another, I don't believe it—like with the car keys. Maybe I get an answer, but I think the Universe is joking.

Maybe to hear the answer, I have to stop for a moment: the mindless chatter in my head, the busyness of my body . . .

Stop! Listen!

So when on a recent Saturday morning, I found myself all weepy and asked what was going on, I stopped. I listened. And I had this miniscule sensation that what was going on was related to loss. I decided to pay attention to this sensation, to accept it as the answer that it was, and I realized I still miss my dad, who died a couple of years ago. As soon as I recognized this, I felt closer to him and the tears subsided.

And when last week I was dizzy and couldn't walk from one place to another without bumping into objects solid enough to make me wince, I asked again, "What's going on here?"

This happened to be the day before we were to take a four-day jaunt to Chicago for a family graduation. I didn't have time to be dizzy: I was washing clothes and packing; buying groceries for the teenagers who would be left behind; paying bills and getting cash; finding just the right graduation card and present and wrapping it; accompanying my son who has his learner's permit and is driving to and from school in one town and his new job in another; picking up the cat's medicine and dosing him; making phone calls for church; and for eight hours that day, working at the office.

"What's going on?" I asked, headed for the car and my next errand.

I got this tiny flash that the dizziness was the Universe's way of helping me perform each task more slowly and deliberately so that my head would have to stay in the same moment as my body. For a split second, I argued, "No, that's silly . . ."

The car keys jangled in my hand. "Okay, maybe so."

By the time we reached Chicago the next night, errands all done, the dizziness was gone. As we got out of the car to greet our grandson, I asked my husband, "Do you have the keys?"

Smiling, he held them up, and we locked and shut our doors.

God is where
you need God

God is where you need Him or Her . . . and when . . . but you have to recognize God when She or He appears. Too often, we don't.

Our family has a favorite story about the preacher who lived along a river when a flood came. A man of God, he believed he had to trust God in everything.

Sometimes it's not our belief systems that are wrong.

Sometimes it's our interpretation of the events around us that's out of whack. Sometimes? Most times!

This preacher looked out his door at the rain and the rising water and prayed to be safe in God. He knew he could count on his Creator, and when a congregant in a Jeep arrived to pick him up and drive him to higher ground, the preacher said: "No, thank you. My trust is in the Lord." And when the Red Cross volunteers came in a rowboat to take him, the preacher waved them on too.

Later, as the water rose, the preacher climbed to the roof of his parsonage to continue praying.

A helicopter flew overhead and dangled a rope for the reverend to grab, but again, he declined, because God would provide.

Well, of course, the preacher drowned and later that day, at the pearly gates, he had a beef with God.

"Where were you? You were supposed to save me!"

And God answered, "I sent you a Jeep; I sent you a rowboat; and I even sent you a helicopter!"

The preacher had visualized God's answer in a certain way and missed the answers God had sent.

Too often we miss God's answers to our prayers. God answers, but God talks God's language. It's up to us to translate.

I seek ways to pass this understanding on to the next generation—yet another need—and God even provides here.

There was this summer afternoon in June.

My daughter—too young to work, too old to stay home—asked me to take her first to the grocery store, then to a friend's house. The friend lives, to use the vernacular, out in the boonies, on a back, back road in the middle of the county. It is a long trip for one as busy as I am.

But my daughter does not drive yet, and I realize that we have not been spending much time together on the days of her last summer without a job.

So I agree, thinking to myself, Well, we can go to the grocery store on the same side of the freeway where the friend lives, and I'll save a little time and gas that way.

After we've packed the car with freshly purchased groceries and other goodies, I think about my itinerary: I had planned to drive back east to the freeway, head north, and then turn back west, retracing my steps.

"Do you know a shortcut?" I ask my daughter. She has traveled with her friend's father and knows this part of the county better than I do.

"Yes," she answers, looking at me just a little warily.

Yes, she says, we could leave the parking lot heading west to begin with, then turn north. My daughter says she's pretty sure she can direct me. A few months ago she got her temporary driver's license, and I know that there's nothing like learning to drive that makes a youngster aware of the roads, and so I think my daughter probably has been paying attention.

Now comes the wary part. "But," she asks with a gulp, "if I'm wrong, will you be mad at me?"

This child of mine is way ahead of the game when it comes to enumerating the risks and calculating the consequences.

I pause to answer that question inside my head, and I realize that this is time I'm enjoying spending with her. Whatever happens is okay. I turn to look at her. "Nope! Let's go for it!"

And we do.

We're cruising along and I can even feel, by the afternoon sun on my left arm, that we're headed in the right direction. Then we come to a dirt road, and she's sure that we should take it. She remembers her friend's father taking it. No hesitation so far. We continue.

We should be there soon, I say, patting myself on the back for trying this new route. The dirt road starts out well-maintained, with large homes here and there, then tapers into a smaller passage, with homes every mile or so. We've been driving quite a while, but I assure her—or me— that all dirt roads lead to paved ones, eventually.

Now we come to the end of the well-maintained dirt road, and there is no paved road. There is, however, a fork.

God, have you been listening? There's supposed to be a paved road here. Highway 16, to be specific. Where is it?

No answer. My daughter and I look at each other. She's trying to see if I am keeping my promise. "Which way?" I ask. My daughter answers, "Turn left . . . I think." And we do.

Although the sun is shining today, this has been a week of flooding and creeks are still high and muddy brown. We see one to the side of the road, and then, up ahead, we see it spilling across the no-longer-so-well-maintained road in several places, and I am ready to concede that, maybe, all dirt roads do not lead to paved ones.

"Let's turn around and retrace our steps until we find someone at home in one of these houses," I say aloud. However, I think to myself, there have been no signs of activity at any of the homes we have passed. I am dubious. I wonder if we will have to backtrack our entire route.

I pull into a rocky driveway and out again, headed back toward the fork in the road, or even toward the original grocery store. I am pondering this when I hear, from behind me, the sound of gravel crunching and water splashing. I look in my rearview mirror, and there it is: the familiar chocolate brown UPS truck out here in the middle of nowhere.

I stop the car. I lean out the window. I holler as loud as I can. "Help!" I know that a direct and insistent entreaty is called for.

The driver pulls up her truck and stops. "What's the problem?"

"We're lost! Do you know how to get to Highway 16?"

"Straight ahead," she calls back. "Follow me." And we do.

Of course, the dirt road eventually does lead to a paved one, and after we honked our thanks to the truck driver, my daughter turns to me and says with a twinkle in her eye, "I didn't know God drove for UPS."

Rising through the cracks

Sometimes it's hard to let life be. Sometimes, for me, everything—from the major to the minor—gets in the way of living in the moment.

Watching the Rwandan children dying in their parents' arms . . . watching my children forget, for the umpteenth time, to pick up after themselves.

Everything—from the major to the minor.

At times such as these, I look at my life and see only what I should be doing more . . . or better . . . or different.

A better parent would have figured out a way to produce neater children. A better world citizen would have known exactly where on the globe Rwanda is located.

One antidote for these times when I'm hitting myself over the head is to remind myself to *let go and let God.* Usually I can repeat this affirmation a few times and feel my dissatisfaction begin to ebb.

And then, one day when I was out walking, God drove the point home with a one-on-one-show-and-tell lesson.

I was headed west down a side street when there, within those few millimeters of dirt between black asphalt and concrete curb, I spied a plant. A woolly, yellow ragwort—I learned later from my wildflower-identification guide.

I marveled at the audacity of this solitary flower that sprouted, grew, and bloomed without regard to how or why or what next.

It simply did its thing, expressing light and life and the love of God right there in a crack at the side of the road. The next car might amputate its golden head, but it let go and let God shine through.

A sigh slipped out of me and I felt lighter.

That's all any of us are supposed to do: express God's light and life and love wherever we are planted.

But, when I got home, I still made my kids put away their bicycles.

Bully wind blows in adolescence

I sat there in the school parking lot, waiting for my son to retrieve a forgotten English book. He had homework, and we had almost driven off without it.

Knots of kids decorated the sidewalk in front of the junior high in Early Adolescence—my least favorite period.

My thirteen-year-old was taking his time, so I found myself watching the youngsters act and interact against the March wind, which blew so hard that the flag's ropes clanged incessantly against the metal pole.

For several minutes two kids tried to still the rope and stop the noise—in vain. Chalk one up for the wind.

Then I saw another kid take his notebook binder from his arms and place it on a bench.

Big mistake.

The same bully wind that taunted the kids with the flagpole now flipped open the binder and blew dozens of sheets of notebook paper across the grass.

Mother that I am, I wanted the boy to run after them. But, at thirteen, running after blowing papers is not something cool dudes do. The young man just stood there and watched.

I saw a young lady approach and take in the situation.

Oh, good! I thought she would come to his aid. She was a girl, and girls generally aren't judged poorly for caring about lost schoolwork. She walked on.

Hmmm.

Next came two boys, one of them twice the size of the other and with a voice twice as loud. They recognized the binder boy and Big Guy bellowed: "Hey, George! Your papers are loose!"

For some reason, all three boys thought this remark was hysterical, and their laughter formed a camaraderie. Well, I thought, maybe now all three can go after the papers leap-frogging across the lawn. Certainly three guys together couldn't be judged sissy for picking up papers.

Sure enough, the Big Guy walked around the bench, bent down, picked up three or four of the nearest sheets, and returned to where George was standing. He held them out to George, and then, as George reached out to take them, Big Guy pulled them back and let them loose.

The wind howled with delight as it caught and launched them a second time. Everybody laughed, except George, who stood there trying to squeeze out a grin and join the joke.

I wanted to jump out of my car, stomp over to where those boys stood, and give them a piece of my mind. I wanted to scold them for their lack of compassion, for their phony "cool," for their blasé attitude about litter.

I wanted to make them grow up right then and there. Skip thirteen and fourteen and fifteen because I couldn't stand to watch them play it out before me. It hurt too much the first time.

Then it hit me. It's hard to watch other people go through their lessons, especially lessons that are painful.

Maybe adolescence is like the March wind that comes in like a lion and goes out, many years later, like a lamb.

You never forget the roar.

Breaking through boards and barriers

There must have been eighteen days in the week between the last Saturday in November and the first one in December. At least. That was the week before my husband was to break boards, for the first time, during his Tae Kwon Do testing.

By boards, I mean pine-tree parts—as in two of them, sandwiched together. Two for the foot. Two for the hand.

Now my husband is an adult and if he wants to slam body parts into boards, well, I guess that's his business. But, frankly, I was worried. What if he slammed his hand into wood and broke it? His hand, that is . . .

I could tell he was a little nervous too.

He attended every single Tae Kwon Do session that week, staying late to practice hitting and kicking some plastic contraption that supposedly simulates board breaking. (You don't get to try breaking wood until the actual test.)

His teachers worked with him. They encouraged him. They assured him he could do this. That's good, because he wasn't getting much encouragement at home. I've never understood this martial-art stuff. I wash his uniform; I even bought him a new one for his birthday, but that's about the extent of my support.

Fortunately, he doesn't need much more from me.

He had wanted to learn Tae Kwon Do ever since his children were grade-schoolers and took karate classes for a while.

Then, one spring, he talked his now-teenage son into attending Tae Kwon Do classes with him two or three nights a week at a local karate academy. I saw it as father-son bonding and a chance for him to finally have a stab, kick, or punch at that longtime desire.

(Not to mention that it left me home alone with the remote control for an hour or two.)

Soon the bimonthly testing started, and I watched as father and son progressed through white, yellow, green, and blue belts. Two months ago he came to me with a red belt cinched around his waist . . . and an announcement that he would soon be breaking boards.

I must confess I was not at all unselfish.

"How will you make water filters with a broken hand?" I asked, referring to one of his jobs at our family business.

"How will you vacuum the house with a broken foot?" Pardon the pun, but I didn't want to wait on him hand and foot.

He said, "I'll be fine."

And he was, up until that last eighteen-day week.

Actually, he was pretty fine then too. Except for all the practicing.

And I started to feel a little more hopeful. Drawing on my limited knowledge of quantum physics, I assured myself that everything is made of moving molecules: all he had to do was slip his hand between the molecules. I told myself that others had gone before him without mishap—or cast.

Saturday came. I awoke early and washed his uniform. He left about 9:15 A.M. as testing began at 10 A.M., the same time I was supposed to be at the bowling alley with our other son for his youth league.

I don't think I even wished my husband good luck. (I certainly didn't tell him to "break a leg!") What he didn't know was that I intended to be there in time for The Attempt.

I arrived at 10:30—to the green belts sparring. A few minutes later the red belts were called to break their boards. I sat there, in the front row, conjuring up every spiritual practice I could to send energy forward.

I was surprised at my nervousness, and I wasn't feeling selfish anymore. I just wanted what he wanted—pine kindling!

Then, there he was, up front. My forty-something husband carefully positioned the boards. He feinted a few blows, first with his hand, then with his foot.

(Oh dear, he intended to use his right hand.)

Then, following Tae Kwon Do tradition, he called out: "Ready for board breaking, sir!"

I held my breath. He sliced at the board.

Nothing.

I held my breath tighter.

He tried again.

It was a most satisfying crack that turned two boards into four.

Now he focused on his foot.

A front kick to the doubled-up boards netted first a thud, and then, another delicious crack.

I breathed again.

And clapped.

Sometimes we build things up to be way more than they are.

We create our own obstacles to crash through.

A pine board isn't a barrier unless we make it one.

I went home and got out the vacuum.

Principles of kayaking

Children, money, and sex can make a marriage, or break it.

The same goes for canoeing . . . or kayaking.

My husband and I have been together for some time now, and we have managed quite successfully to negotiate the rapids in our relationship without ever picking up an oar.

The few times we have floated the Buffalo National River, we rented a raft. Rafts are the bumper cars of the floating scene. You don't need to steer. You don't need to paddle. You don't need to instruct your spouse, "Not that way!" or "Watch out for that branch!" or "You're going to tip us!"

You get in the raft and it takes you where you're going—gently down the stream. And merrily, merrily, merrily you get out at Kyle's Landing . . . or wherever.

So it was totally out of character for my husband and me to sign up to go floating in a two-person kayak where the guy in back steers and the gal up front takes pictures and, maybe, occasionally sticks the tip of her paddle in the water.

But then being in Sitka, Alaska, was totally out of character. (It was my parents who cast us in this scene: they invited their children and spouses to celebrate their fiftieth anniversary on an Alaskan cruise.)

So there we were in a raft, motoring to a bay where the kayaks were waiting when my husband pointed out that I was just about out of film. OH, NO! I looked at my camera and learned I had only three pictures left.

Only moments before my brother-in-law had turned to me and said, "I'm counting on you to take pictures now, because we didn't bring our camera." And the guide had told us to expect to see, at the very least, a sow and her two bear cubs.

My stomach churned.

(Understand that these are the kinds of things that can wrench my guts. I can handle broken bones, broken water mains, and broken hearts much better.)

But I've not been on the spiritual path for a few years now without having picked up a few helpful tips. So I asked myself, as we crested and fell over waves in the raft that was taking us farther and farther from any drugstore, "How do you apply Truth principles in this situation?"

Principle Number 1: You let go. Even of the small things.

You let go, and you trust that the answers will come.

I let go. And almost immediately I thought to ask a fellow passenger, who had a camera case hanging from his neck, if I could borrow or buy

film from him. He said he would check to see if
he had a spare roll when we got to the dock, and
I relaxed for the rest of the ride.

When we arrived we put on our flotation vests
and listened to a presentation on how to maneuver
a kayak through salt water with an ambient tem-
perature of 32 degrees. I watched the guide with
the front of my eyes and my Potential Film Source
out the sides.

"I have a roll," said PFS.

Thank God!

Principle Number 2: Maintain an attitude of
gratitude.

Relieved, I memorized his cabin number so
I could replace the film later on the ship. By now
the talk was over, and my husband and I headed
to our kayak.

He got in first while I finished putting the new
roll of film in the camera. I started to get in when
both he and the guide hollered at me.

"Sit down!"

Well, guys, that's what I was trying to do.

My husband hollered again.

"Sit down on the dock! Sit down and lower
yourself into the boat."

Oh! Okay.

Settled in, with camera between my legs and
paddle across my lap, I was all ready to venture
forth when from the backseat of the kayak comes
this disdainful, word-for-word, complete and un-

abridged replay of the guide's instructions—liberally sprinkled with editorial comments such as, "Obviously you weren't listening."

I got so mad I turned around and called this man every unprintable name in the book.

How dare he accuse me of not listening!

How dare he be oblivious to my frantic search for a roll of film with which to take pictures of the #$!*! brown bears he'd been waiting to see the whole trip!

How dare he!

In his favor, he had the grace to sit there quietly and not jump out.

And then I became aware that I was going to be spending the next two hours two feet in front of this man I married. Hmmmm. It seemed I had a choice to make.

Principle Number 3: The only moment in which to experience joy is this moment now.

I could stay aggrieved, or I could let go of the anger (having vocalized every last ounce) and enjoy the $47-a-person outing. Another Truth principle at work: We are free to choose.

So we rowed, rowed, rowed our boat, and the trip was like a dream, except the bears didn't show! I used up twenty-four frames of film with shots of people, boats, trees, and one starfish . . . but no bears.

Later, on the dock, I recounted what had happened (safely out of my husband's earshot) to my sister and brother. I was trying to make the point that we choose our attitudes, and of course, I had to repeat what my husband had said to me in the kayak.

"What a turkey!" my sister said, grinning.

My brother, however, looked puzzled. "He was only trying to help out since you obviously didn't hear all the instructions," he countered.

Principle Number 4: Perspective is everything. You always need to take into account where the other person is coming from. In this case, the men from Mars saw it quite differently than the women from Venus.

Indeed, everything is relative, and for the sake of the relatives, the three siblings laughed, declared a truce, gathered up spouses, and went off to buy some film.

Dueling voices

I jumped into the family van for the short jaunt to church. It was Sunday morning, and traffic was light to nonexistent. I didn't bother to put on the seat belt.

Along the tree-lined streets on this fine summer day, people began emerging from their air-conditioned burrows to fetch the morning paper or to get into their own cars and head for their own churches or temples or, maybe, just to go eat bagels.

I'd driven a few blocks when I was ready to recognize that my seat belt hung limply behind my shoulder. My daughter was not along for the ride, or I already would have latched it across my chest. It's not that my daughter needs a role model. She always wears her seat belt. No, what I need to provide her is validation that she's right about this one: Seat belts are to be worn on every trip.

Why, these words had poured from my very own lips for years when my children were toddlers and grade-schoolers.

Oh, I'm not driving very far, I said now to the memory of those words. Immediately, a little voice inside my head reminded me about an article I'd just read of a man who was permanently injured in a car crash. He was not wearing a seat belt. He said he had thought to himself, the morning of his life-changing trip, I'm only going two miles.

"Come on! I'm trying to scare myself," I said aloud, trying to laugh the discomfort away. I was almost to my first destination, to pick up my husband who had driven ahead of me so that he could drop off my broken car to be fixed Monday. Then both of us were headed to the church.

"You really ought to put the belt on," the little voice badgered me.

"Well, I'll probably have an accident if I try to put it on while I'm driving," I answered it.

Wouldn't that be ironic?

"Isn't that rationalizing?" asked a Higher Voice.

Gee, it was getting hard to think with all of these voices.

I thought that I could put on the belt when I got to the automotive repair shop. But then came some voice from somewhere: "This is silly. I almost always wear my seat belt. Why am I making such a big deal about it this morning, the one time I don't wear one? I mean, how likely is it that I'm going to be in an accident this one time?"

When my husband got into the van, he didn't mention the other passengers. Perhaps because they were invisible.

But I'm the kind of person who is willing to introduce everyone, and my husband is the kind of person who understands my weirdness.

I looked at the street, saw no cars, and decided to execute a three-point turn and be on our way. I hit the gas and sped across the street, stopping just inches from the curb. Then, shifting the van into reverse, I pulled back quickly, shifted again, and lurched forward. Three sharp points.

My husband yelped.

"Are you trying to test your theory?" he asked through clenched teeth.

I laughed and said, "Look, Honey, we're on our way to church."

"And God will make sure we don't get into an accident? Is that what you're saying?" he asked.

Gee, yet another voice.

"Well, if I'm one with Spirit, then can't I trust Spirit to keep me accident-free?" I countered. "I mean, God's will for me is good, and it can't be thwarted by my wearing or not wearing a mere seat belt, can it?"

Then, addressing my Higher Voice: "What kind of God would let me crash on my way to church?"

"Look," It answered, "I'm staying out of this. But you already know the answer to that one."

The road to church was winding, the kind my little car—the one in the shop's parking lot—maneuvers easily. But, in the big hulk of a van, the vehicle careened as I took the curves.

"Hey!" came the voice from the seat to my right. "I don't want to crash just so you can test your theory. Maybe this time your little voice is the one you ought to pay attention to!"

At last! A worthwhile purpose for the little voice.

Still, I had to wonder whether God's will could be thwarted by my wearing a seat belt or not.

"Okay," came the Higher Voice. "Here's a hint: God's will for you is good. God's will for the whole world is good. But, wisely or not, and I'm editorializing here, God gave the world a will of its own, and if anyone's doing any thwarting . . ." The voice trailed off.

I paused for a moment.

Okay, God has given me the little voice—and the Higher Voice. God has given me a strong-headedness, and God has given me a sense of adventure. God has given me curiosity, and intelligence too.

God has entrusted me with all of these gifts. My job is to use them in a combination such that the gates of Heaven can open up, right here on Earth, and let God's will shine through, showering me with my own good.

God would be there in the middle of a wreck.

God's already here in the middle of the nagging.

How I meet God is my decision, not God's.

"What are you doing now?" my husband asked, as I flipped on the turn signal a mile from the church.

I turned onto a side street and stopped.

"You drive," I said, as I got out of the van. Then, settling into the passenger seat, I put on my seat belt.

My husband followed suit.

Keeping the High Watch

By the time I was seven months pregnant with my firstborn, I had quit my job and was hanging out at home—in more ways than one.

We lived on five acres on the edge of town, so there were hosts of squirrels and birds and bugs as well as my white cat Stomper to keep me company while my husband was at work. Stomper loved the woods almost as much as I did, and he spent most of his time outdoors, especially in the spring.

One such afternoon while napping on the couch, I awoke to a tumultuous commotion outside my window: a crashing of branches and high-pitched squawking. I sprang up to see what was the matter.

I was aghast.

There, in the front yard, was an angry blue jay dive-bombing my cat, screeching at him, using all his birdly powers to get the cat's attention because Stomper had the jay's tiny baby in his mouth.

I joined the jay in screaming at my cat. I chased him, tried to catch him, but Stomper ignored me too and disappeared under the deck to a place I could not follow—even if I had been seven months smaller. The adult jay finally gave up, flew away, leaving me standing there alone, shaking.

Suddenly I understood the pain of parenthood. In less than two months, this baby inside me would be out of its shell, and like the father jay, I would not be able to keep him from all harm.

Did Mary feel this when she held her babe in arms and Simeon prophesied that Jesus was destined "to be a sign that will be opposed . . . and a sword will pierce your own soul too."

Luke's Gospel mentions several times how Mary watched what was happening with Jesus and how she "treasured all these words and pondered them in her heart."

Is that the destiny of parents? To watch?

We help bring these beings into human form so that the world can ravage them as well as delight them. Watching them laugh is easy. Watching them struggle is hard. Watching them fail is excruciating. How am I to deal with my children when they are not laughing? How much am I to intervene? Should I go screaming after them, following them into dark, tight spaces?

These are the thoughts I ponder in my heart as I watch my firstborn child, sixteen years later, face down the tigers of "teendom."

Do I warn him of the prey, or do I just pray? I do both.

But I've come to believe that the best thing,

the most important thing I can do as a parent is to keep the High Watch over my child. To do what Jesus asked of his apostles in the Garden of Gethsemane—to wait and to watch. To see the situation through God's eyes.

To let go of the human anger, frustration, and pain, and to know that, even in the most perilous events, God is there, keeping watch too.

I see my Christ-child son, whose chameleon face flashes from wily grin to scowling mask when he spots me looking his way. I see and understand his whole and perfect journey down a God-ordained path. I see him making it, eventually.

I keep the High Watch over him—God's watch—and I am blessed to do so.

4

Shifting From Fear

to Trust

You are a child of the universe, no less
    than the trees and the stars; you have
    a right to be here.
And whether or not it is clear to you,
    no doubt the universe is unfolding as
    it should.

—Max Ehrmann, "Desiderata"

Ally ally oxen free: We can come in now

I was twenty-six and stretched out across the couch with my boyfriend. We were looking out the window at the night sky, his arms wrapped around my shoulders, his mother's quilt wrapped around us both.

I stared at a radio tower in the distance, with its three red lights on a vertical tower. I was hypnotized by the incessant blinking . . . on . . . off . . . on . . . off . . . on . . . all night long. The tower stood like a sentry, guarding the night sky.

My boyfriend whispered to me, "I want to be your sanctuary." That's when I knew I wanted to marry him and be safe.

Over time, the safe feeling dissipated, but to this day, when I see the red tower lights blinking, I feel warm and protected. Sanctuary is something I've been seeking all my life.

As a child, I felt safe. Protected. Snug as a bug in my upstairs bed on Saturday morning, while, downstairs, my dad scrambled eggs with chives, and my mother set the table. I could hear their conversation drift up through the floor register, and I used to wonder how I would ever live in a house without someone older there to protect me at night.

When my dad died, it felt like my cloak of protection had been jerked from my shoulders. He hadn't been able to keep me from painful lessons during my childhood or adult years, but his loving presence gave me a certainty that I would survive . . . and feel safe again.

My baby brother, now in his forties, had a stuffed lion he called Gooey that watched over him all night long. One morning I walked into his room to find Gooey's shredded foam stuffing all over his crib. It was a brave act for a two-year-old.

My stepson, when he was four, threw his Linus blanket onto a luggage carousel at the airport to watch it go around with the suitcases, except that the moving ramp caught the edge of it and swallowed it forever. My husband still remembers the astonished look on his son's face.

My son uses pets to simulate Gooey and the blanket, and at seventeen, he still sleeps with our cat beneath his bed covers. My daughter has a favorite comforter (there's truth in advertising) that accompanies her to every slumber party, and every bedroom around our house.

I see New Age folks with crystals. I see Catholics with scapulars—I wore one for years. I see the well-rubbed belly of Buddha statues. I see Jews with mezuzahs on their doorposts. I see the Unity "Prayer for Protection" printed on wallet-sized cards.

In the face of fear, does God just give us symbols? How much power can these symbols have when they can, like the blanket, be yanked away at a moment's notice?

Maybe it's time to recognize that we are the ones who give power to the blankets and the bears and the statues and the stones. Without our attachment, they're as powerful as lint.

And what is the power that we give to these things? It's the power to make us feel safe, secure, loved.

Somehow we have to move from giving the power away to outer symbols to fanning the Energy inside, where an infinite supply of security, safety, and love exists.

If I have the power to say that a husband or a parent or a blanket can keep me safe, then this must mean that the power lives inside me, and I already am safe and secure and loved.

We can't give away power that we don't already have.

Ally ally oxen free. It's safe. We can come in now.

Riches by the roadside

You drive along the road these summer days and the wildflowers are a sassy assortment of colors and textures and shapes. The regal Queen Anne's lace towering above the fat, pink sweet-pea blossoms. The orange daylilies that got loose and ran away from long-ago yards. The stalks of blue chicory.

You have to pull over and stop to see the smaller blossoms.

The paintbrush tips of the burgundy clover. The glossy, yellow buttercups. The flashing sparks of red from the fire pinks.

We would call these weeds if they were in our backyards.

I used to stop to pick these flowers that, with the passing weeks of summer, changed their names and shapes and colors. I gathered them for my dinner table, my bedroom, my living room.

No more.

Somewhere along the way, I stopped. Not because I wanted to, but because something inside me had changed.

My need to cut and keep the blooms, to own them for myself—conflicted with my prosperity consciousness. What we put out, we get back. We are all connected by the divine Spirit.

There can be no ownership—only a flow of riches to and from and all around.

This has been an understanding long in coming for me, and I have to remind myself of it each summer when the first flowers reappear by the roadside. I find myself looking out the window longingly. Where are those clippers anyway?

The urge to stop and pick and possess is still there.

But I can own them without possessing them.

So I tell myself they are mine because I've seen them, and my living room becomes the stretch of highway from here to distant towns.

I claim these blooms for me, but I let them remain ours: flags by the asphalt, riches by the roadside—left standing so that others, too, may claim them as they pass.

Finding lost treasure

They carried their two-year-old to the water's edge, and gingerly, the mother stepped into the small metal rowboat. She sat down on the bow seat, and the father handed her their daughter, dressed in a white summer cap and sunsuit. Then, shoving the boat into the water, he jumped into the stern of the craft, using the oar to push off into the rippling lake.

The mother placed the two-year-old on the boat's bottom, where she was within reach of either parent's arms.

Too short to see over the side of the vessel, the child contented herself with inspecting a smooth stone found on the bottom of the boat. She rolled the cool stone in the palm of her hand, glorying in its roundness. She was too young to worry about how to use it in a game, too young to need to gather more to keep forever. The stone alone was enough.

And when she finished her exploration, she looked up and watched as clouds scudded against an ocean of sky. She didn't search for pictures in the clouds. She didn't try to determine the speed of the wind. She didn't wonder if the white wisps portended rain.

The clouds were clouds. It was enough.

There, in the boat, she lived that afternoon, safe and content.

It was a memory to last forever, and it should have been enough.

So, how come now, dozens of years later, the memory remained but the feeling did not?

How come now, clouds brought rain and stones bruised her feet as she walked across town in sandals?

How come now there was no time for contemplating stone and sky?

She pondered this on drives to work . . . while waiting in lines at grocery stores . . . when balancing the checkbook.

And her answer began with the recognition that one doesn't look for something that's lost until one needs it.

She needed it.

Where to look?

When she was young, the nuns had taught her a prayer to St. Anthony: "Tony, Tony, look around. Something's lost and must be found."

Now, in the middle of middle adulthood, she still used the ditty to find car keys, receipts, and overdue videos. Sometimes she even loaned the ditty to her friends. Tony batted well over .800, but could Tony help her find this intangible? The thought made her smile, and she knew she was getting warm.

And on the next drive to work, she remembered the ride in the rowboat. What was so different about the stones and clouds back then?

On the way home, she realized that she wasn't expecting anything from them.

The next morning, as she put away groceries while juggling the phone on her shoulder and waiting for the pasta water to reach a boil, she realized the mindfulness of herself at two. The moment was all there was, and the people and objects that filled it were all that mattered.

Later, when she was balancing the checkbook, she realized how in balance she was at two. How heart and mind and soul acted as one entity. Not separate from each other. Barely separate from her parents.

Not separate from the Source within creation, although she didn't have a name for God back then. She had a feeling, though: safe.

She finished reconciling her register against the monthly statement, and then, rather than go online to get her e-mail, she shut down the computer and headed for the yard.

Along the way, she grabbed her trowel. She spent the rest of the day digging in the dirt, coloring her yard with the flats of flowers she'd bought earlier that day: orange and yellow marigolds, flame-red salvia, and tiny purple lobelia blossoms.

The dirt caught under her nails and wouldn't wash out in the hose spray. Her back was stiff from bending. But when dusk arrived, she realized she was smiling.

She looked up at the orange-sherbet clouds, melting in the setting sun. She looked down at the stones by her feet.

She stretched out her arms and found all the treasure she needed, enough to assure her safety forever.

She threw back her head and laughed out loud.

Take me to the dentist

I asked my Higher Self to take me to the dentist this summer. I hadn't been there in years. It was a money thing. I needed thousands of dollars' worth of work, and I didn't want to invest that much energy in my teeth.

I figured it would be cheaper to let them fall out and replace them with dentures.

The last time I'd gone, I'd been able to trade a whole-house water-filter system for the work (our family business makes these), but how many whole-house water filters does a dentist need? I didn't go back.

Shortly after that, I started applying spiritual principles to my teeth . . . Tried to heal them with affirmations, hoping for a miracle.

It didn't get me the results I'd hoped for, but it did help keep everything together until I came upon a better alternative to dentures. Dental insurance.

When I left the family business to work for someone else, the someone else offered great benefits—including dental insurance.

The way I figured it, dental insurance would cut my costs in half. But, after all these years, I was fearful of what the dentist would say when I did go.

Months passed and my only action was to pay the premiums. Then, in what could be seen as a first step, I sent my kids to the dentist last spring.

When, however, the pain in my jaw began to show up on a twice-weekly basis, despite my affirmations, rinsing with saltwater, and dabbing with tea-tree oil, I knew it was time for me to call for an appointment.

Then fear and shame surfaced.

I didn't want to go to the dentist to have him tell me how bad it was that I hadn't come in before now. The thought of sitting in that chair, listening to loud noises, and having an authority figure chastise me was almost too much to bear—even with dental insurance.

That's when I realized I could ask my Higher Self to take me.

She did. In fact, She did such a great job that She headed things off at the pass, explaining outright to the dentist that he didn't need to comment on how I had avoided treatment in the past because, frankly, what mattered was my commitment to undergo treatment now.

The dentist listened to Her, then proceeded to clean my teeth.

I felt my body tense. I was trying to brace

myself against the pain. And there was my Higher Self again, reminding me to relax my muscles, slow my breathing. I came to envision the chair and its arms as the arms of my Higher Self, supporting me. Within thirty minutes, the ordeal was over and I was still waiting for the pain. It never came.

Then the dentist X-rayed my teeth and gave me the bad news. There were to be several visits in store for me, beginning with a root canal. I'd never had one of those, but I'd heard horror tales. My friends said, "Be sure and get some good drugs."

The dentist said, "Take an Advil."

Instead, I took my Higher Spirit, a Walkman, and a David Lanz tape of piano music to turn up to full volume when the drill was at its noisiest. It turned out to be an incredible experience. I remained in an alert but meditative state the entire time.

I was fearful of pain, but my Higher Self assured me we'd figure out something. Turns out, there was no pain. Even the needles bearing novocaine were barely felt, and afterward, there was no soreness.

Using the two hours in the chair to relax, listen to music, and stay centered, I was in an altered state when the dentist finally pushed the tool tray away from me. I pulled off my earphones.

"Bad news," he said. He said he had not been

able to stop the bleeding in the canal so that he could dry it out and fill it with the resin that would support a new crown. I was going to have to come back for a second visit.

"Sure," I answered. "No problem."

And I meant it.

There's my miracle!

Backing up my life

I've had a computer mentality since I was a little kid and giggled at the initials IBM. Like the experienced computer operator of today, even then I wanted to back up everything.

When I found a dress I really liked, I wanted to buy another just like it to have when the first one wore out.

When I splurged on expensive perfume and got to the last quarter inch in the bottle, the fragrance would go bad before I would let myself use it up.

To this day you can give me a box of Good 'n Plenty candy and I'll drop some pieces into my top drawer so that a few of the licorice morsels will be nestled among my scarves long after the rest of the box is devoured.

I wanted to back up things because I couldn't find a guarantee that there'd always be more of what I wanted—or thought I wanted.

If I couldn't have any guarantees, then I'd make sure I had backups. In my finances. In my jobs. In my relationships.

Even as a child, it made me vehement to see trapeze artists perform without safety nets.

No one was going to catch me without one.

But it's hard to have a backup when you work for yourself in your own business.

It's impossible to duplicate a good spouse.

And God doesn't send out carbon copies (the original backup) of children, an example of Divine Order if ever there was one . . .

Given all of these one-of-a-kinds in my life, I came to regard money as my backup.

"God, if you could just stick a couple hundred thousand into my bank account, it would make it so much easier for me to be a trusting soul."

I know better now . . . well, I almost do.

This last month has been a tightrope walk without a net.

I've lost a best friend, a best friend-employee, and temporarily at least, my sense of family.

My friend called me to say we couldn't communicate anymore. He's going through his own hard times. (Luckily, I still have a couple of backups in this category!)

My friend-employee said she would have to quit working for health reasons. (No backups here!)

And my visit to see parents and siblings left me feeling like an alien. Always before, I'd go out, shift gears, and have fun for a week. This time I stayed in my own head space, argued with them, cried to myself, and wondered if I was adopted.

I came home trying to let go of the fear that I was losing people and things I couldn't replace . . . and contemplating how to fill the voids.

I stayed quiet for a while, in my own head space. If I was going to be walking this tightrope without a net, I was going to need to stay in balance.

And in this quiet, calm place, my "bestest" friend—Spirit—communicated with me, promising to fill whatever voids develop in my life . . . to catch me if I fall . . . to be my very own top-drawer source of God 'n Plenty.

Hiring the right voice, using the right tools

I've been living with my family in an apartment for the last five years. Often, during this time, I have wondered if I'd ever live in a house again. And when.

Now, eight weeks into building a home for us, I see Divine Order in the timing.

Clearly, I needed several years of meditation and God affirmations under my belt even to attempt this work of heart. And I'm not sure even several years are enough.

One has to collect the necessary tools to build a house, and I'm not talking saw, nails, and hammer. One has to hire the appropriate supervisor to oversee everything.

After years of subservience to a critical inner voice that lives inside my head, I refused to hire her for this project. Unfortunately, she's ignoring the "No trespassing" signs I've erected and butts in on a regular basis.

Nevertheless, I have turned over the control to my Intuition. She's acting as General Contractor, but sometimes she's hard to find.

When I can't locate her, I have to remember that I need only to calm myself and get centered, and then she will step forward, equipped with all the necessary tools to make all the necessary choices.

Her tools are as nonconventional as she.

For example, she doesn't need to use a hammer as much as she pounds away with perseverance—fitting the pieces together in solid fashion. And, rather than attacking the hard places with a saw, she cuts through them with the understanding that everything is happening as it should.

Her tape measure bends to fit the nooks and crannies of the project, and her safety glasses see only the positive dimensions of this time.

Sometimes it's hard for me to use her tools.

Swing after swing, I hit myself on the thumb because I just won't move my hand.

I had wanted to build this project perfectly, without mismeasured windows, without left-swinging doors that should have swung right, without arguments with my husband, without children telling me they wanted bigger bedrooms, without a budget—or with a bigger one.

We have ordered glass too tall that then had to be installed sideways. We have had to put the furnace on the second floor rather than under the house. We have gone overbudget on several line items.

Reflecting on the last two months, I find it telling that my eyes focus first on the mistakes.

I need to borrow my contractor's special glasses because, with the house standing, roofed over and glassed in, obviously, a great deal has gone right.

Maybe, with all the wrangling, reordering, and hand-wringing, just maybe the house is being built perfectly.

In the meantime, my General Contractor reminds me, "Blessed are the flexible, for they will not be bent out of shape."

Not perfect

The top of my husband's desk is papered in bills—for lumber and lights and carpet and cabinets. Material costs of the new house.

I spy them and sigh.

"Trust that the money will be there," comes a Voice from inside. I take a deep breath and let it out.

The story of the loaves and fishes comes to mind: how the Apostles started handing out one small basket of food and ended up with leftovers, after feeding thousands.

That's all I ask, Lord.

We've been in this housebuilding process since November, and it's been a lot like giving birth. In the midst of labor, you swear you'll never do it again. I'm swearing.

There's been a lot of letting go too.

Letting go of having to know ahead of time where the money's coming from (we're still in the mortgage-application process). Letting go of needing to have things exactly match the images in my head, although the carpenters might argue this point, as many times as I've asked them to redo walls, windows, and what-nots to suit my taste.

Letting go of expecting other people to know

what I want or need—and letting go of needing to have them provide it. They have their own needs to meet.

Letting go of needing to find perfection in me and in others. This last is a real beast. If I can't have something perfect, I can go into a really dramatic "Then-I-Don't-Want-It-At-All!" tantrum.

"Sell the house!" I yelled to my husband in the middle of one such fit.

Wisely, he did not, and now we're in our new home: unpacked boxes on the floors, closets in need of modular shelving, a kitchen cabinet or two still in the garage.

Not the way I planned it, but we're in it.

Not finished perfectly, but we're in it.

Kind of like my life.

Not the way I planned it, but I'm in it.

Not happening perfectly, but I'm in it.

I'm in it, trusting that the whole experience will teach me what I need and provide me what I want.

And when I remember to stop and sit quietly for a while, perhaps on the back deck where the trees sway to the wind's beat, I close my eyes and the Voice asks, "What could be more perfect than this?"

I say good-bye,
I say hello

On the morning a young coworker of mine sent her son off to kindergarten, I sipped a cup of coffee and ate a biscuit and egg at Burger King while watching my uniformed son, now out of school, dust the recessed light fixtures in the ceiling.

I called out to him, because there was only one other occupied table in the restaurant. "It's good to watch you working."

He replied, "Are you saying I'm usually slacking off?"

"No. It's just good to watch you working."

Then, smiling contentedly, I threw away my trash and headed out the door. He probably watched me from the top of the ladder, shaking his head, but I didn't look back.

My son is making his way in the world now without needing me to propel him out the door— to school, the doctor's office, the ball field, the emergency room, the library, the driver's license office, the first job.

Yes it was with a thrill and an ache that I

dropped him off at kindergarten all of those years ago, and I did look back. As they say in the soda-pop commercial, "Been there, done that."

His high school graduation a few months ago pushed me into a pool of reminiscing. I pulled out all the baby albums. I looked at old video-tapes. And then I cried when I saw a young mother pushing her infant in a stroller down the street.

I'll never do that again, I thought to myself, and an ache began forming in my throat.

Geez, do I really want to do that again?

Well, it would be nice to flit back and forth in time, so that I could spend a day nurturing babies and then, later, return to the present and take them to the pool without worrying all day long about whether or not they're drowning.

And I do remember how difficult it was to push the stroller down the cracked and bumpy sidewalk. So why the ache?

"Why, indeed?" I asked myself on the first day of this fall semester, when my son was awash in Windex and his younger sister was brandishing a brand-new backpack at the high school down the block.

She'd chosen to make her entry into tenth grade on the arm of a friend, so the two would have someone to eat with at lunch.

There are new adventures in store for each of my children—and for me too.

If I can say good-bye, then I can say hello.

As if this was not enough to deal with, I had another good-bye in store the very next day. My husband and I were signing the sale papers on a small apartment complex we owned downtown. We'd lived as a family in this complex for several years while we nurtured a fledgling business. Moving into an apartment among our tenants—and out of the home we owned on the outskirts of town—had been a big good-bye in its own right.

The move turned out to be perfect, of course.

That first night in the apartments all of those years ago, the two of us sat outside on our porch and looked around as our tenants barbecued, waved hello and good-bye, drove off, and came back. We listened to the church bells chime. And we knew we were going to love living downtown.

We moved out of the apartments five years later, after the family business had matured enough to let us build a house. We built it two blocks from downtown!

Last year I took another job in another town and no longer had the time to devote to caring for the apartments. My husband, now without my daily help at the office, didn't have the time either. We opened ourselves to the possibility of selling this piece of property that was supposed to be our retirement security.

It was a risk to let go, but our hearts were no longer in it.

Our memories were, and they came flooding back the morning of the sale.

My kids grew up around those apartments, etching initials in the wood stairs, hiding GI Joe figures in the dirt, coloring the parking lot with chalk drawings. I'd left candy canes on all the doorsteps at Christmas, colored eggs at Easter. My husband had an intimate relationship with every patch of poison ivy on the property.

We'd known a bevy of young men and young women whom we had alternately befriended, policed, and parented. We said hello when they arrived with cartons and clothes. We said good-bye when they left for new adventures.

Now it was our turn to say good-bye.

As we walked into the bank that morning, where the closing papers awaited our dozens of signatures, I took my husband's arm.

If we can say good-bye, then we can say hello.

Perceived absence of light

An astronaut, talking to a congregation in Florida, described his epiphany in space. Looking out the shuttle window, he saw only blackness.

Yet his scientific mind knew that light was everywhere. The galaxy is filled with stars that burn brightly, reflecting their essence.

The light was traveling so fast, however, that his eyes could not perceive it. The astronaut had to satisfy himself with knowing it was there, even though his human body would not verify this truth, and when he finally returned to planet Earth, behold, there was light.

It's that way even if we never step into a space capsule. We have to know the Light is there even when we're groping in the dark. It's that way for me.

During adulthood, I have suffered on and off from depression. In my early adulthood, I used therapy and antidepressants and found my way out. Later I added a successful marriage to the successful therapy and drugs.

By the time I hit middle age, I found my spiritual roots and a church family and figured I was home-free. No more depression for me. In times of stress (which typically precede my depressions), I would tell myself to just *let go and let God*.

That's what I tried to do this past winter. Stressed out over family, work, and even church issues, I had assumed way more responsibility than God intended, so I tried to hand everything back to the Almighty. Except I couldn't seem to find God. I'd pray and get voice mail. I'd meditate and hear only my own chatter.

Still I hung onto my belief that God was there, much like the astronaut who knew that light was around him.

God was all around me, but my flailing arms would not be still long enough to be encompassed. I surprised myself: I thought my spiritual awakening in recent years would keep me free of any future depression. But when my daughter, who has seen the mental-health ads on TV, asked if I ought to check in somewhere and get happy, I realized that all the affirmations in the world were not crosses I could hold up to ward off this depression. I was going to have to plod through the darkness once again.

What was I to do this time? Intuitively I knew that whatever I decided would need to have a spiritual dimension. Affirmations, meditation, and other prayers would be a part of any regimen.

But I think the most important aspect of my

treatment was to remember—morning, noon, and night—that my depressed perception was not the Truth of who I was. Like the astronaut, I knew the Light was present. In my case, it was I who was moving too fast to see it.

With the assistance of a winter virus, I slowed myself to a halt last month. Now, as I start up again, I move more slowly. I also pulled a few of my favorite things out of a time-tested trove of feel-good tricks: music playing loudly, pots of blooming hyacinths, hot steamy baths, homemade soup simmering on the stove, morning walks, movies that make me laugh out loud, and friends who don't screen my calls.

In the end, as spring renews itself in the backyard of my house and in the atrium of my heart, I know that what was most important about this little voyage was knowing, even in the darkest shadows, that the Light was always there.

God does not go away, and neither can I.

5

Fixing All

With Love

we're anything brighter than even the sun
(we're everything greater
than books
might mean)
we're everyanything more than believe
(with a spin
leap
alive we're alive)
we're wonderful one times one

—E. E. Cummings, "if everything
happens that can't be done"

Jesus needed to make a human connection

Did Jesus need anyone? Did he need his mother's unconditional love? His father's approval? Peter's loyalty? Mary Magdalene's affection? If not, then why did he arrive here as an infant? He could have just dropped down, full-size, from the sky, like an alien from a more spiritually aware universe and taught us the same lessons—with a lot more authority.

But I think Jesus needed his human heart so that he could connect with ours. His message had to be understood from our inside out.

So he showed up as a baby, needing a mother to feed, clothe, and hold him. Needing a father to teach him how to read, handle a saw, and say the blessings over the Sabbath wine.

I think he needed people too, after he became a young man, although The Gospels don't mention much about the give-and-take between him and his friends. Perhaps he let the little children come unto him because he needed their pure, unquestioning acceptance to make a point about how adults should act.

He assumed the human condition was all about making a human connection, and that meant he had to let himself depend on people, to need people. He needed the masses to hear him. He needed his friends to help him in his work, to trust him, to respond to his message . . . to reflect him.

What he needed in a friend is not so different from what we need. We don't need friends to make us whole. We need friends to help us— caught in these incomplete human forms—to see our sacred wholeness. We need friends to hold up a mirror so we can see ourselves more clearly.

And, just as important, we need our friends to let us hold the mirror right back. We stand there together, in a symbolic undressing room, looking into mirrors reflecting mirrors reflecting us. And when we put down the mirrors, we take away a new vision, a different perspective, maybe even an appreciation for something in us that before we had ignored, feared, or belittled.

I want to spark you to walk with greater confidence, laugh more from the heart, see farther, and appreciate the connecting of our souls, and I want this for me too. Isn't this what Jesus was trying to do with his friends? To inspire them to a more joyful, peaceful, purposeful life?

Jesus was a mirror for his friends to look inside their hearts, find the Truth of what he spoke, and go for it! And he needed them right back. He needed them to look or there wasn't going to be any point to his human trip.

And he, in his all-too-human form, needed them to reflect back love. Do you think, when Mary wiped his feet, he sat there without appreciating how good it felt and how sweet the costly ointment smelled?

Jesus needed his friends to express their caring in many ways, from taking him boating to sharing meals to staying with him that last night in the garden, even if they did fall asleep.

Although he might have understood his friends' behavior that night (they were sleepy after the sumptuous Passover feast), don't you bet he was disappointed in them . . . and in Judas who betrayed him . . . and, later, in Peter when he denied their friendship? Friends jump ship, sometimes—even the best ones. Still, the connection remains.

And that's why Jesus needed to assume the human condition. He needed his friends to help him with a lot of things over the course of their time together, but what he most needed them for was to demonstrate this: Despite any outer appearances, our many hearts are united in a holy bond that can never be torn asunder.

Settling my "car-mic" debt

I'm not the first student of Truth to know that inside an automobile is one of the hardest places to stay on the "straight and narrow path."

When the car ahead stays stopped ten seconds after the light has turned green, I feel a dark force pulling my palm toward the horn.

When a tractor-trailer rig turns wide and I have to back up and the driver behind me has to back up and the driver behind him has to back up, that's when I scowl and vigorously shake my head.

When pedestrians saunter across the street, totally oblivious to the line of cars accommodating them, I want to roll down the window and yell at them to get their blankety-blanks in gear.

These are the times that try my soul.

I catch myself getting angry in my car mostly when I, obviously a considerate person, have to slow down to accommodate some other driver, obviously an inconsiderate person.

And speaking of consideration, do you know how inconsiderate traffic lights can be? Anytime I'm late for an appointment, they all turn red!

Tom Crum, Colorado aikido master and author, once said that drivers take it personally when forced to stop before arriving at their destinations. It's as if that traffic light saw us coming and, quickly turned red.

Crum, however, suggested seeing the stop as an opportunity to re-center. Take a deep breath, be still, and know that God is going on, right in the middle of that intersection. Hmmm. It's pause for thought.

I have come to think of cars as litmus paper that tests the evolution of our spirituality, and I'm beginning to think I should ride the bus!

Until recently, I was finding it easier to deal with inconsiderate traffic lights than drivers. Then I had a narrow escape on a narrow street.

On my way to work, I was headed west when a car pulled out from a driveway, turned east, and then decided to turn a sharp left in front of my advancing car. I slammed on my brakes.

We were close enough to read each other's faces, and I was ready to lay on my horn when I recognized the man. He was someone I used to work with. He was someone I like. He was someone like me.

I pulled back my hand and smiled as he looked at me with a sheepish grin and drove on.

Hmmm. I slowed down to think on this. How come I flipped from anger to understanding in that fraction of a second?

Clearly, I was in the right. Clearly, he was in the wrong. Clearly, except it no longer mattered because when I recognized the driver for who he was, I was suddenly willing to accommodate him.

Maybe his driving behavior did convey the message that his time was more important than mine, but if he had known who was coming down the street, I think he would have stopped and waited for me to pass.

And if I had known the truth of who he was, I would have willingly slowed to allow him to turn first.

It seems that when I recognize the Truth of who the driver in the other car is, whether I know him or not, I don't mind the ten-second delay in getting to my destination.

If I can be this understanding of my friends, can I not be so with strangers too? Didn't a wise wag say, "A stranger is someone I haven't met yet"?

I know Jesus said, "I was a stranger, and ye took me in." Maybe, today Jesus would say, "I was late for Temple, and ye let me go first at the four-way stop."

Hmmm. Maybe if I just plan on seeing the Divine Essence of every driver within a 100-foot radius, I'll find my blood pressure a little lower, my brakes lasting a little longer, and my "car-mic" debt a little more settled.

What time is it right now?

This is the last time in my life that I will be doing this, I think to myself as I move the car forward another vehicle length. It's the final week of junior high for my daughter. Next year I won't have to navigate this daily snarl of traffic, created by parents dropping off teenagers too young to drive, too old to be caught riding the bus.

We're in the school's driveway now, and I scoot the car in next to the sidewalk and behind a parked car—it belongs to a teacher, my daughter tells me.

She gathers her backpack, her purse, and her cup of Dr Pepper (poured over my objection that she should be drinking milk), says "Bye" and is gone.

I'm left stuck behind a car that's not moving, having to unparallel park my Ford Probe in an ocean of moving teens, minivans, and sport utility vehicles.

I crane my neck over my left shoulder and wonder if the sea will part and God will repeat the miracle. A man in a red Explorer gestures to me to move out, and I do. I smile and wave. There's a different savior every day in the Woodland Junior High School parking lot.

The tide of vehicles moves slowly, gaining momentum—and then we spy the city garbage truck that's stopped ahead, wanting to wade in. The tide stops, the truck turns, and I marvel at the patience of all of these drivers at 8 o'clock in the morning in the school yard.

I marvel at *my* patience.

Put me in line anywhere else—on the highway, in the grocery store—and you won't find me merrily waving people into line in front of me. I've got to get where I'm going—fast. So does everybody else, it seems.

At school, it's different. At school, we all see each other as parents of students who need to be dropped off, picked up, and otherwise, cared for.

There, in the school parking lot, we see that we're all in this together—this being the 8 A.M. and 3:15 P.M. traffic cycles of which we're part.

So we work together to keep vehicles moving along, everyone waiting a little so that no one has to wait a lot. We let people in. We wave and smile. We move forward.

Within a few minutes, we're on our ways again. Free to ignore pedestrians patiently waiting for a break in traffic to cross the street. Free to run the yellow-turning-red light because it was too short, and we're too late. Free to forget that we're all in this together—this being the 8 A.M. to 8 A.M. life cycle of which we're part.

Later that night, I'm sitting in the bleachers in the baseball stadium, cheering on the college team. A crowd of 4,000 has come to support this team, which within the next week could win the conference championship.

My husband and I find our seats, but they are filled already by students who want to sit right behind home plate. There are empty seats in the third row, so we choose not to make them move, unless our new seats' rightful owners show up. They do not.

The mascot, wearing a baseball uniform, comes over to start tossing candies into the crowd. Hands spring up to catch them, then, often as not, to share the treats with those nearby.

A ball is fouled to right field, and I watch a snarl of bodies leap skyward. One man snags the prize, smiling widely as he twirls it in his fingers. And then, he makes a gift of it to the ten-year-old girl beside him, wearing a baseball glove.

I marvel at our generosity. Here, in this sports stadium, we understand that we share a common bond. We act upon this bond. We understand that our emotions are all tied together. We cheer, we clap, we groan.

And when the home-team batter sails another ball past the wall, we jump to our feet and whoop, as if we shared one body.

But if that body bumps into us in a crowded elevator, will we frown with irritation?

It's becoming clear to me that we already know we are all connected. We choose the times and places when we admit it, recognize it, act on it.

And we choose the times and places when we forget it.

What time is it right now?

"Tail" of two kittens

My son recently spent a week volunteering at the animal shelter. The second day on the job, he called me.

"Mom," he said in his most pleasant voice, and he has several, "I want to ask you something, and I don't want you to say 'no' until I've finished.

"If I walk the dog every day and clean out the litter box and feed all the animals and take out the trash, can I have two kittens?"

Our family lives in an apartment, and besides two parents and two to four kids (we share custody with other parents), we have one cat, one really big dog, forty-three fish, and one red-eared turtle. That's not counting the three squirrels we keep in sunflower seeds.

"Son," I respond in my most understanding voice, and I have several, "how about you bring one kitten here and the other to your dad's where he has five acres and a barn?"

I'm feeling smug at turning a no into a yes when he counters, "Oh, Dad's already promised to take two other kittens."

My son spends a week at the animal shelter and wants to bring all the animals home.

No way, son. No way we can have two more kittens.

He calls the night before his last day of work.
"Please, please can I have two? I can't pick between Silent Sam and Little Caesar."

He'd already named them.

"No." I'm firm.

He hangs up on me.

The child calls me back later and threatens to be just awful if I don't let him have two kittens.

I calmly tell him that hanging up on me and making threats are not the most persuasive tactics.

But, now, he explains his dilemma—how he has come to select these two out of dozens and how he can't pick between them and how it's tearing him up to know that the one he doesn't choose likely will be euthanized. I'm beginning to melt.

I ask for guidance and hear myself saying: "Bring both home, and we'll see how it goes. If it's too hard, we'll have to find another home for one of them."

So Sam and Caesar join our clan and bring us so much joy that I am happy to have them here—even with their providing a daily supply of fertilizer, even with the Kitten Chow circlets crunching under foot, even with the veterinary bill for distemper vaccinations and feline-leukemia tests.

One Friday morning, the phone rang. The vet was on the other end. He said Sam's test for feline leukemia was positive. Feline leukemia is fatal. Most diagnosed cats can live six, seven, eight months, maybe.

We can retest Sam in a few weeks to be sure, the doctor said. In the meantime, we have to keep him isolated from other cats.

Caesar is too young to be vaccinated against feline leukemia, and vaccines aren't foolproof anyhow, the doctor noted.

I send out a prayer for a negative test next time or strength to accept another positive and the right words to tell my boy.

Heart heavy, I close up Sam in our bedroom, Caesar on the other side.

Black velvet paws stretch under the door and are met by soft gray ones.

The kittens must be separated even more, and Sam is moved to our office.

I look at my husband, and we wonder how we will make it through these next few weeks or six or seven months. We wonder how people live their last weeks when told they are going to die.

We think about this, and we talk about how we will cherish each moment we have with Sam, filling it with love and peace and laughter.

Loving him now because he is dying soon.

Then my husband asks two questions.

"Why does it take death staring us in the face to make us show our love?" And, "Can't we spend every moment loving everything as if we only had that moment left?"

We can, and maybe, that's Sam's gift to us.

We all go to heaven

I wasn't there when he lost his first dog.

Alex was a red cocker spaniel given to him by a friend who was going through a divorce and who could not keep the pup in his new quarters. (Alex was hyperactive—as most cocker spaniels are. I kept my distance.)

I wasn't there because I was in California, sharing our infant son with my parents.

He called me.

Alex had been hit by a car.

He sobbed. I cried—and tried to reach through telephone lines to comfort him.

It got all tangled up.

He buried Alex alone, planting a sapling atop the small hump of dirt. A dozen years later, the tree stands watch over the garden.

We didn't get another dog. We had an infant developing into a toddler—enough activity for the both of us.

A few years later we had a daughter. And then we had a divorce.

When the children were older, he heard about a blond cocker spaniel in need of a home. The spaniel was blind in one eye.

And so Fluffy entered his heart and the hearts of our children.

"Killer dog," he would joke, because Fluffy would take after any moving shape, expecting, I suppose, to catch it and nuzzle it to death.

I kept my distance: I didn't live there anymore, and he and I were not able to share emotions—they got all tangled up.

About two weeks ago I was alone at his house, awaiting children, now much older. They would be stepping off the school bus at his house and riding in the car to mine.

Fluffy had escaped the fenced backyard and came to check on who was sitting out front. I took my hand, and for the first time ever, petted him.

His head of curly hair, full of knots tied by the wind, was firm beneath my hand. Solid. Comforting. I petted him and remembered how my daughter had shown me that if you pet him, he would not run off to chase the next squirrel, bird, or bus that came whizzing by.

The school bus came, the kids got off, and Fluffy stayed beneath my hand.

Yesterday afternoon no one was petting Fluffy when a car whizzed past the house. The children called, sobbing. I reached through the telephone lines to comfort them.

"If only we'd kept him behind the fence," they cried.

I had no answer. I asked God for words, but God said: "Words get all tangled up. Just do your best."

"Fluffy was a free spirit," I said gently. "He

reveled in roaming the five acres, from creek to road. Now he's chasing clouds in the fields of the sky."

"Will he come back as another dog?" they asked.

"If he needs to," I replied, "but he's here right now—in you and your dad, and even me."

Breathed from the mouth of one God, we're all connected.

We all go back to God.

We all go to heaven when we die—and every time we connect in love.

Model parenting?
Not exactly

My husband likes to tease me about how we're running a home for wayward boys. Not exactly. I'm not your model mother, by any means. Still, I find that having two teenage sons and building a house that has an entire floor devoted to them has been a male magnet.

When our eldest son moved away, his room became home to a friend of my then sixteen-year-old son. We took him in, and after a brief cocooning, he moved on to Tennessee. This year we took in a seventeen-year-old who, after a few weeks, returned to his own mom.

Still, my son's friends come 'round regularly, including the one now living with his mom. There's many a night I find him sprawled across the floor. I wake him long enough to shove a pillow under his head.

There have been other young men who have spent nights on our floor. And I have wondered why they are here. Is it because I'm the easiest mom around, the one who puts up with their innocent and not-so-innocent shenanigans?

Is it because I pretty much leave them alone or because our freezer is stocked with breaded jalapenos stuffed with cream cheese? Maybe it's that I let them play Metallica at volumes that scare cats into closets.

Why they come around probably has to do with all of these things—the stuffed jalapenos, of course, being more heavily weighted.

In any case, I find myself asking God, "What is the lesson here?" You see, my son isn't the child I thought I'd have. Not exactly.

This doesn't disappoint me. What it means, rather, is that I'm not sure how to mother him. This son of mine marches to the beat of a different drummer, and he has a rhythm section of like-stepping friends.

I know that they are all expressions of God, but it's disconcerting to me that many of them know what the inside of a courtroom looks like, and not from civics class. They wear the same clothes two or three times a week, and all of their possessions can fit into a maximum of two trash bags. They know which stores will sell cigarettes to minors, which older friends will buy them liquor.

None of them go near the high school after 3 o'clock.

My son and his friends are different from their classmates.

After being "trash-canned" in junior high by people he thought were friends (that's where kids gang up and stuff you in a Dumpster when no teacher is nearby) and ignored by those he knew were not, my son befriended others who felt as alien as he.

When he does share thoughts with me, it's in short bursts: maybe when we're driving to school or while he's standing in front of the microwave oven waiting for the jalapenos to heat.

And when he does talk, I have to listen carefully, practicing restraint, and seeking niches where I can tuck morsels of advice.

Perhaps that is my best attribute as his mother: listening. Perhaps, but often my critical self taunts me: "I am too easy. I understand too much."

Some things my son tells me frighten me. He likes to see himself as "living on the edge." He smokes cigarettes. He's haphazard about homework; he thinks school is meaningless. His vocabulary is X-rated. His bathroom stays buried in wet towels and dirty clothes.

"I should be doing more," I chide myself. "I should be disciplining him by taking away the car, withholding his allowance, prohibiting friends' visits."

I begin to fear that I am doing this mom thing all wrong.

And then my heart answers: "Perhaps I doubt myself too much."

What do I want for him? Do I want my son to have only the lessons I would choose? Do I want him to be more conforming so that I am more comfortable?

Maybe, but that's not why he's here. Not exactly.

He's making his own choices, and sometimes he still talks to me—more than in monosyllables.

For all his arguing about how "bad" he is and that "it's everybody for himself," when I told him his sister was crying after his friends had teased her for being so "straight," he went to her room and comforted her.

When his best friend needed money, my son shared his job with him. Now he's looking for a new home for his guinea pigs because he doesn't think he's spending enough time playing with them.

His actions belie his words.

What would I pass on to my son? To quit smoking? To eat more broccoli and fewer tacos? To just say no? To go to college? To hang up his towels? To save money? To have safe sex? To take vitamins? To drive carefully?

I'd choose all of these things for him in a minute, but they don't make up the real legacy I want to pass on. Not exactly.

What I want is for my son to know that we are all connected: we of his family, we of his school, we of our town, our state, our nation. We of the world. We of the universe. We of the Spirit.

Wait! That's not right. Not exactly. I don't mean for him to "know" this; I mean for him to remember what he was born knowing, at some deep and sacred level.

The rest of it is just lessons on the road to remembering.

My job as mom isn't to hurry him along. It's to help him hear his inner voice and to trust it.

To pass on this legacy, I need to model it myself. Exactly!

Life's Littleton lesson

*W*here I work, as a copy editor on the night desk in a newspaper office, the television set sits on a filing cabinet just above my right shoulder. The set is turned on for such things as news conferences, football drafts, elections, and ballgames. We also use the TV to monitor breaking news. From the moment I walked into the office on Tuesday, April 20, 1999, until midnight when I left, the Littleton, Colorado, nightmare played into my ears.

My consciousness is different now from twenty-five years ago when I was a reporter. When I heard about the high school shooting in my car on the way to work, my first response was to utter a prayer reminding myself that God is in the middle of everything that happens—even horrendous tragedy. And I prayed that the community would recognize the Presence as well and that those who were injured would be able to tap into God's healing power.

My second response was pain.

I knew that this shooting was a tragedy—one more in a chain of eight school shootings across the United States in less than two years. I knew it was a tragedy by the way my insides lurched when the TV camera caught the boy who, with his limp and bloodied arm, dragged himself out of a second-story window and fell into the arms of the waiting SWAT team. The anchorman brought home the reality—and the finality—of the day with one simple statement: "Fifteen people won't be home for dinner tonight."

The girl with the twice-pierced eyebrow—and the sound of her voice full of tears and terror—is memorized in my mind. She looked into the eyes of the boys who shot the people around her and found no way to reach them and stop the insanity. Neither she nor the hundreds of other teens in the halls and classrooms at Columbine High School could touch these boys now. They had disconnected themselves from every other human being, and—in the end, as they committed suicide—from themselves as well.

I listened to the people around me: the editors and reporters, the pressmen and the mailroom clerks. I heard them cry that adults had allowed these students to have access to machine guns, grenades, and bombs. I heard them wail that no one inside the school had been able to disarm the youths.

I heard the county sheriff blame the media for its coverage of school shootings, and I was reminded of how human it is to want to kill the messenger who bears bad news. I heard Colorado teenagers stumble about, trying to find answers as to why this happened so they could explain it away and feel safe in school again. The shooters were outcasts, they said. Trench-coat mafia. Never did fit in.

The TV reporter asked the teens if the shooters went to dances and ballgames and the like. The prom was just last weekend, and, no, they weren't there, the survivors answered. They weren't connected.

My daughter called me at the office, after watching the television coverage, and asked how come they didn't realize that, if we all come from God or Adam and Eve or some original mother, they were hurting their very own family.

They didn't feel the connection, I answered.

That is my only answer. It doesn't begin to address the pain or the anger. But it is enough answer for me.

A quarter of a century ago, I would have wanted more answers. Why, God? Why is this happening? And I would have tried to explain away the tragedy, to distance it from the sanctuary of my life with answers like, "There's too much violence in the movies, on television, and in video games" or "We live in a society where people will die to protect their right to guns" or "Parents aren't strict enough with their kids."

These things may be accurate, but added together, they do not sum up the Truth: When we feel our connection with each other and with God, we live in love and peace.

In our individual lives, I believe we have lessons to learn, and there's a theme to these lessons. The lessons keep coming at us, increasingly harder, until we learn them. My husband said to me that the human race may have lessons to learn as well. And until its collective consciousness figures out how to deal with them from a place of love and peace, the lessons will keep coming, fast and furious.

How many school shootings have we had? And workplace shootings too? Does the Universe have our attention yet?

I think the very fact that there have been so many shootings (ironically, at a time when violence in schools has decreased) has forced us to drop the pretense of trying to package answers into neat little bundles.

Our nation has been stunned, staccato, so many times now that we are seeing the uselessness in trying to find some tangible talisman we can hold tightly to keep tragedy and pain at bay. We are beginning to understand that the answer cannot be found in paper laws and concrete jails.

We are coming to look inside ourselves for an answer that has no physical substance, but one that can manifest itself within a hug, a smile, a conversation.

I find hope in the President coming on television to say there was no way to make sense out of this senseless tragedy and, instead, quoting Paul who wrote in his first letter to the Corinthians that we can only see through the glass, darkly. We can see only a small piece of the big picture. That's our limitation as human beings.

That's our blessing too. How better to demonstrate connectedness than in small pieces, by looking at, by seeing, by loving—one person at a time.

whose voice is
in my head?

It was halfway through our work shift when I started to tell my colleagues some silly joke. I don't even remember it now. I do remember the voice.

In the middle of telling the story, I heard a familiar little voice in my head chastising me: "What makes you think they're interested? They probably think you've been talking too much. Don't you have work to do?"

I forgot the punch line.

That little voice and I go way back.

I used to think it was my mother's voice, moved into my head, but my mother would never be so unkind to anyone, much less her firstborn daughter.

Still, it does have a motherly quality to it—the nagging mother, the mother who promises she's telling you all of these things because no one else will, the mother who just wants you to be your best . . . but, of course, there's always room for improvement.

"I just want you to be safe," whispers the little

voice, trying to rationalize its harsh and biting words.

I used to buy into that. Well, okay, I still do. Sometimes.

But, when I can hush the voice long enough to ponder what's really going on, I realize that the little voice's primary goal is to keep itself safe—which it thinks it can do by keeping me safe, limited, and afraid.

If I don't try new things, I won't get hurt, and the little voice keeps its job.

If I discover that I can do stuff I'd always dreamed of, then I may never again pay attention to the little voice.

The little voice tries to keep me in line, afraid that if it is lenient with me, I will turn into a wild and unpredictable creature.

I am as good as I am because it taunts me into submission: that's its main gig.

I wonder if I could enroll it into some job-training program to prepare it for another career. But its work experience, unfortunately, is limited to telling me when I'm eating too much, driving too fast, ignoring my seat belt, talking too loud, or having the audacity to think I can do something that's really special.

"You! Write a book? Hah!" it scoffs. "Lots of people think they can write a book. What do you have to say that hasn't been said before?"

"You write too little," it yips when I wrap up the story in a one-page essay.

"You write too long," it yaps when it takes two sheets of paper to finish the thought.

"You should have spent more time on that. It could have been better."

Sometimes I think I need the voice. To keep my writing sharp. To keep my house clean. To keep me considerate of other people: "Don't you think you should call them? They haven't heard from you in weeks! What kind of friend are you anyway?"

The voice is arguing for its very survival.

So am I.

I'm old enough now to recognize that it's not the voice of my mother, although she may have had a similar one living in her head that slipped into mine somewhere along the way.

Some days I wonder if it's my daughter's!

On the first day of spring, my daughter and I were walking down the street when I spied some children playing in front of the library. They were running back and forth, shouting "Boo" at each other in between their giggles.

"Boo!" I called out to them as we passed.

"Mother! Really!" came my daughter's voice, sounding ominously familiar. Is this voice a product of heredity?

Maybe the voice does serve a purpose in our

lives—for a while. Maybe it gets us through early adulthood when mortality is a fuzzy concept. If I could tuck the voice into the head of my son for a few years, I certainly would! He's nineteen and still living at home, upstairs from me. With his loud music, fast car, mountain biking, cave exploring, cigarettes, eyebrow, ear, and nipple rings, he could use a little restraint.

And yet, some afternoons, as the ceiling reverberates with Pink Floyd from his stereo, I find myself vibrating to his freedom. He has lessons to learn, but at least he seems not to be limiting himself with verbal taunts and self-jeers.

Perhaps the little voice served me well in the years when I was exploring who I was and what I wanted to be when I grew up. The choices were myriad, and it helped me limit them to a manageable number. I had to really want something to ignore the voice's negativity and go for it: the day I talked my boss into my first reporting job, the year I was elected to the county legislature, the moment I admitted my marriage was over.

I used the voice as a measuring stick: if I could jump over it to reach my goal, then that goal must be worth the risk of failure. Not that the little voice admitted defeat—it would get in gibes meant to keep me from overly enjoying my successes. "Won't last," it warned.

Now, though, in middle adulthood, my knees aren't into jumping hurdles. I don't need this self-limiting inner voice any more, and yet (like my son) I can't seem to get it to move out!

Could I, perhaps, get it to move downstairs—from my head into my heart where I can soothe away its fear and where I can forgive it?

Jumping ship

Sometimes it's really hard to tell on myself, but I will. My husband and I have a family business that makes water-filtration systems for home and business. One of our popular products is a filter that screws onto the end of a shower pipe and removes chlorine from the bathing water.

In the beginning, our business had a problem with some of these filters. In certain areas of the nation, they would clog and, occasionally, their plastic casings would split. Customers called to complain.

In our business, we tot up the bottom line with these principles: we are all one in God, and God—not our customers—is the source of our supply.

From this perspective, we talked with the customers who called. We were positive, pleasant, and ready to replace their filters—for free. We trusted that the money to keep on providing the filters, and to keep us in business, would continue to flow.

Most people were pleasant right back. But, once in a while, someone read us the riot act, and we had to sit there, listening—without getting anxious or angry—and then, calmly try to satisfy the customer.

This was, and is, hard for me. I take failure so personally, assuming responsibility for any mistake within 100 yards even while shrugging off successes as dumb luck. (I think I'm missing something here . . .)

As a consumer, I've watched a lot of products fail and not received any relief. I have a Formica kitchen countertop that discolored immediately and the manufacturer, after initially agreeing to replace it, has since ignored my calls and letters.

I have a rebuilt engine, with a three-year warranty, in my van that has broken down twice in the last three months. I have windows in my new house that leak. I have a squirrel-proof bird feeder that the squirrels demolished its first day out. I have a computer monitor that won't stay on—without a toothpick stuck next to its push button.

I've learned to live with other people's failures. So why, when my stuff fails (and we even replace it!), do I want to hide?

Do I really think I have to be perfect to be worthy of God? Am I lacking in the faith that God loves me, regardless of split hairs, split infinitives, or water filters?

Sometimes I fear that God just sails in the middle of the good stuff—and jumps ship when things get rocky. But what about the story of Jesus in the boat?

In The Gospels of Matthew, Mark, and Luke,

Jesus is napping in a boat that his friends are navigating. It's evening. A storm comes up. Waves start crashing over the vessel's sides, and the fisherfolk are stressing out big time.

My guess is that, not only are they scared, they are feeling like failures. After all, these men are supposed to know their way around a boat. All Jesus had asked of them was to let him rest awhile. He'd had a busy day, and he was tired.

Now there's this tempest, and the guys in charge can't steer through the raging waters. Not only that! This boat represents their livelihood. Without it, they can't fish!

So they go get Jesus, who is in the stern of the boat—head on a cushion, fast asleep. He certainly epitomizes the calm in the middle of the storm.

They wake him: "Save us, Lord! We are going down!"

He sees the terror in their eyes, and he asks them: "Why are you so frightened? You have so little faith!"

Nevertheless, Jesus gets up, rebukes the elements, calms down everything, and astounds the apostles.

They marvel, "Who is this man, that even the wind and sea obey him?"

The apostles are agog, but I'm beginning to think they missed the point here. The point isn't that Jesus practiced weather-control techniques or that he happened to be in the right place at the right time. It isn't even that he was Jesus, per se.

No, I think the point is that Jesus, and we, too, carry the Calm within—regardless of whether it's fair sailing or rough seas. That calm is the presence of God . . . the faith that Divine Order is always there.

What else would Jesus have had his friends do that night? While he slept, they hoisted and trimmed sails. They threw in the anchor; they pulled it out. They grabbed the rudder; they baled water. They did everything they knew how to do.

So here I was in a sea of water filters that were clogging and splitting and threatening our livelihood. I'd done everything I knew to do to fix the problem. What was left?

I think that what Jesus was demonstrating is this: When we've done everything we humanly can, and we're still on shaky ground—or sea— it's time to calm ourselves and know that the God within is using this storm as part of the Divine Plan.

We may not know if we'll make it to shore in one piece, but we do know that if we have to jump ship, God will be jumping with us. Jesus understood that. His friends didn't.

Maybe I'm beginning to.

Who do you think you are? God's gift?

When I was a child, I thought as a child. I thought my bedroom was huge. I thought my parents were God, and I thought I was God's gift—for the first few years of my life.

Then came my little sister and my baby brother, but they stayed smaller, so I was still on top, or so I thought.

I was the smartest (straight As), the richest (biggest allowance), and the prettiest (well, Mom told me every day what a pretty girl I was). In short, I was queen of the mountain with no intention of sharing the peak.

Doesn't this just scream hubris?

Younger siblings have a way of dealing with hubris. They grow up. Now my brother lays claim to the title of "smartest," my sister "richest," and both outstrip me in the pretty department.

But I'm on my Ozark mountainside and happy nonetheless. How do I explain this change in my perspective?

Well, I grew up too.

I came to realize that, as adults, we can revisit our childhoods and maybe find there that which we could not as kids.

We can look at our memories with the wisdom and understanding that come with life experience.

For myself, I don't need to revisit my childhood as much as to revisit the relationship I had with my siblings.

There's a lot to be said for growing up as the center of the universe. It makes it easier to accept that one, indeed, is God's gift to humankind. But the realization that comes with maturation is "So is everyone else!"

As a kid, I probably looked down on my siblings because I was unsure there was enough love and respect to go around. Now that I know there are, I have been able to reestablish my relationship with them on a more level footing.

Me, perched in the Ozarks doesn't mean my sister can't ski down her Canadian slopes nor my brother bike across his Sierra Nevada range. There are peak experiences enough for all of us. There is love enough to go around.

Sometimes we have to use our midlife bifocals to see what was there all along.

For example, I had a friend who thought his childhood was tough. His dad became wheelchair-bound, forcing his mother to return to work full time. His siblings were almost a generation ahead of him and living on their own. So by the time he started school, he felt abandoned and wondered about his place in his mother's heart.

When his mother passed on, I helped him sort through her possessions. From a trunk, I pulled scrapbook after scrapbook of photographs taken of him as a child. And in these scrapbooks was page after page of his mother's handwriting. She had recorded all the events of his young life.

I wondered if he could now see how much his mother, indeed, had cherished him.

I have a girlfriend whose siblings were brothers at a time when sons were treated dramatically different from daughters. My friend grew up with doubts about her place in the family.

Then, for Christmas, one brother gave her a copy of home movies taken of her as a baby—a baby showered with love and attention. It was her best gift ever.

My friends are lucky to have such tangible proof that their childhood perspectives were skewed. Their young hearts just weren't big enough to take in all the love that was there.

But whether we have proof or not, it helps to revisit our childhoods through the eyes of the people we are now.

We can better understand how the gift of love that brought us here in the first place has remained constant, because it is God's gift, because it is God's love.

We all are God's gift to the world—and to each other.

It's time we started acting like it.

About the Author

In various orders on various days, Peggy Treiber is a writer, personal buyer, editor, wife, daughter, laundress, journalist, mother, and animal handler—and the last two may be interchangeable. On a given day, she has anywhere from two to five children—biological and step—depending on whether or not the kids are admitting it. Her family is scattered across the world, while she stays put in the heart of the Ozarks in Fayetteville, Arkansas.

Her spouse Jeremy is her best critic (if that's not an oxymoron) and her best friend.

In her spare time, you can find her volunteering at her church or at her husband's temple or lifting weights at the local gym. She does all of these things, she says, because (a) she can't make up her mind what she wants to be when she grows up, (b) she likes to study time issues, or (c) she's a Type A personality who'd like to be demoted to Type B.

Her writing, for which she has won a few awards, explores themes of finding why she is here on Earth and where she left the car keys. Her basic premise is that all creation is connected, and what happens to one, happens to all. Her proof is in the washing machine.

Printed in the U.S.A.　　　　　185-3436-3M-9-01